## DATE DUE

| | | | |
|---|---|---|---|
| | | | |
| | | | |
| | | | |
| | | | |
| | | | |
| | | | |
| | | | |
| | | | |
| | | | |
| | | | |
| | | | |
| | | | |
| | | | |
| | | | |
| | | | |
| | | | |
| | | | |
| | | | |

DEMCO 38-296

# THE WORLD TODAY

Marshall Cavendish Corporation
99 White Plains Road
Tarrytown, NY 10591-9001

**Consultants**
Professor Charles Ingrao, Purdue University
Professor Ronald J. Ross, University of Wisconsin–Milwaukee

Created by Brown Partworks Ltd
*Editor: Timothy Cooke*
*Associate Editors: Robert Anderson, David Scott-Macnab, Casey Horton*
*Design: Wilson Design Associates*
*Picture Research: Jenny Speller, Adrian Bentley*
*Maps: Bill Lebihan*
*Index Editor: Kay Ollerenshaw*

**Library of Congress Cataloging-in-Publication Data**

History of the modern world / [editor, Timothy Cooke].
     p. cm.
    Contents: v. 1. Origins of the modern world—v. 2. Religion and change in Europe—v. 3. Old and new worlds—v. 4. The Age of the Enlightenment—
v. 5. Revolution and change—v. 6. The changing balance of power—v. 7. World War I and its consequences—v. 8. World War II and the Cold War—
v. 9. The world today—v. 10. Index
    Includes bibliographical references and index.
    ISBN 0-7614-7147-2 (set).—ISBN 0-7614-7148-0 (v. 1).—ISBN 0-7614-7149-9 (v. 2).—ISBN 0-7614-7150-2 (v. 3).—ISBN 0-7614-7151-0 (v. 4).—
ISBN 0-7614-7152-9 (v. 5).—ISBN 0-7614-7153-7 (v. 6).—ISBN 0-7614-7154-5 (v. 7).—ISBN 0-7614-7155-3 (v. 8).—ISBN 0-7614-7156-1 (v. 9).
ISBN 0-7614-7157-X (v. 10).
    1. World history Juvenile literature. I. Cooke, Timothy, 1961- .
D20.h544 1999
909.08—dc21
                                                   99-14780
                                                   CIP

**ISBN 0-7614-7155-3 (set)**
**ISBN 0-7614-7156-1 (v. 9)**

Printed and bound in Italy

07 06 05 04 03 02 01 00  7 6 5 4 3 2 1

History of the
Modern World

Volume 9

# The World Today

*Marshall Cavendish*
*New York • London • Toronto • Sydney*

# The World Today

U.S. astronaut Edwin "Buzz" Aldrin stands beside the Stars and Stripes on the surface of the moon in 1969.

# CONTENTS

# Introduction

At the end of the second millennium—as measured by the calendar made prevalent by Western cultures—the world faced a range of problems. *The World Today* shows that some of these problems, such as ethnic or religious conflict, would be familiar to people from earlier centuries; other challenges were new, such as the effects of instantaneous connections among national economies.

The end of the century saw a search in many nations for new forms of politics. Chapter one describes the emergence in the West of a skeptical rejection of institutional government in favor of the power of the individual citizen to affect his or her own environment. Chapter two examines the prosperity, particularly in the United States, that supported advancements in human and civil rights. Chapter four tells how some European states attempted to overcome the limitations of national politics by entering an increasingly formal economic and political union.

During the final years of the twentieth century world-changing influences occurred around the globe. Chapter three describes Mao Tse-tung's efforts to guarantee Chinese communism and the struggle by his successors to preserve the communist system in the face of capitalist business and demands for democracy.

Chapters five through nine show how various regions have prepared themselves for the future. Chapter five describes how many countries of Latin America experimented with military dictatorship before adopting more democratic styles of government. Chapter six shows how, in the countries of the Pacific Rim, economic development and prosperity did not depend upon democratic institutions. Chapter seven shows how in Africa the continued influence of the former colonial powers and indebtedness to the developed world presented problems for dictators and elected governments alike. Chapter eight shows how Islam forged deeper relations between religion and politics throughout the Middle East and in Africa and Asia. In 1989, the communist bloc of eastern Europe began to disintegrate, followed by the Soviet Union itself. Chapter nine explains how, although some former Soviet countries transferred smoothly to new political systems, others fractured into nationalism, crime, and war.

The end of the century brought evidence of both human ingenuity and human stupidity. The technological innovations described in chapter ten improved medical care and communication but also created more destructive weapons and more harmful pollution, as chronicled in chapter eleven's survey of humanity's relationship with its planet. Chapter twelve looks into the future, highlighting causes for both optimism and pessimism and showing how the lessons of history are as often ignored as they are heeded.

*The Editor*

# The Political Debate 1960–1999

*Experiments with Government*

By 1960, the countries of western Europe and North America were in the middle of a period of sustained economic growth that brought unprecedented prosperity to the majority of their citizens. U.S. economist J. K. Galbraith (b. 1908) dubbed the phenomenon "the affluent society." Virtually all Western governments shared similar economic and social policies that accepted the need for government intervention in many aspects of life. Such an approach was a product of the lessons of the Great Depression of the 1930s (*see 8:965*), which undermined confidence in the ability of an

unregulated capitalist economy to deliver prosperity. World War II had also forced governments to take control of many aspects of social and economic life.

Although there were many differences from country to country, western European governments were in general committed to substantial state intervention in the economy. Through tax and monetary policy they aimed to create virtually full employment at the expense of a modest level of inflation, a program known as Keynesian economics for the British economist J. M. Keynes. On average, only around 3 percent

U.S. president Ronald Reagan, photographed in 1984. The Republican Reagan embodied the shift to the right in Western politics in the early 1980s.

of the workforce was unemployed, and inflation averaged around 4 percent a year. Many Western governments also took major industries such as energy production, transport, and communications under state control, a process called nationalization. The state ownership of economic assets created so-called mixed economies that combined free-market capitalism with elements of state socialism.

### The Welfare State

Western European countries were broadly committed not only to maintaining full employment but also to providing for the social welfare of their citizens through state provision of pensions, education, health care, and social security. Different countries pursued such policies to differing degrees. They were taken furthest in Scandinavia, especially in Sweden. Sweden's Social Democrat government created a system that protected and provided for its citizens from the cradle to the grave, with guaranteed education, health care, public housing, and income supplements. Such "welfare states" were expensive, however. They depended on a largely affluent population and high levels of taxation to fund them.

### The United States

The United States never became either a welfare state or a mixed economy. The legacy of the New Deal era of the 1930s, however, ensured that federal agencies intervened actively in the economy (*see 9:966*). Programs guaranteed farm prices by buying up surplus produce, for example. There was also aid for worse-off members of society: social security payments in the United States rose from $960 million in 1950 to $10.7 billion in 1960. In the 1960s, President Lyndon B. Johnson launched a "war on poverty" that included the Medicare and Medicaid federal health programs and expanded federal funding for education (*see 9:1175*).

On a global scale, the welfare capitalism of western Europe and its harder-edged

American version were contested by the Marxist philosophy of the communist states, primarily the Soviet Union and China, which controlled an area stretching from central Europe to the Pacific. In its own way, Soviet communism was as buoyant in 1960 as Western capitalism. Soviet leader Nikita Khrushchev spoke of "burying capitalism" through the superior progress of the Soviet economy. The Soviet lead in the space race in the early 1960s, when the Russians and Americans competed to send an astronaut into space, gave the communist system great prestige.

Although there were powerful communist parties in Italy and France, the model of Soviet communism had little appeal for people in Western countries. It was, however, influential in the developing world, where countries became independent in the postwar period. India, for example, though it was a democracy, had close relations with the Soviet Union and imitated state socialism in much of its economic policy.

This insignia, which was displayed in a town in the Soviet Union, included the hammer and sickle of the Soviet Union and the initials CCCP, which in the Russian Cyrillic alphabet stand for USSR, or Union of Soviet Socialist Republics.

A statue of Lenin stands outside administrative buildings in Saratov in the Soviet Union. Although the Russians' technological advancement seemed in the early 1960s to be capable of equaling that of the United States, it later became apparent that the stagnating Soviet economy had effectively hampered innovation and development.

Thousands of young people lie down in New York City's Central Park in November 1969 in a demonstration against casualties caused by the United States in the Vietnam War.

Student leader Rudi Dutschke, pictured here addressing an anti–Vietnam War rally in Berlin in 1968, was the spokesman for disaffected young Germans in the 1960s.

## Roots of Protest in the 1960s

During the 1960s, radical opposition to the state of society in the Western world developed among a significant minority of young people. Because of a so-called baby boom, the result of a high birthrate of the late 1940s and 1950s, there were exceptionally high numbers of young people in Western countries in the 1960s. A far higher percentage of young people than ever before were students. The United States had 3.5 million students in 1960 but more than six million by 1968. The rise in student numbers elsewhere in the Western world was similarly impressive. It was among these students that radical political ideas fermented in the 1960s.

The 1960s generation of young people was better off than its predecessors had ever been, and students were the most privileged of their age group. How did so many members of this elite come to see their own societies as repressive, unjust, and in need of radical reform or even revolution? To a considerable degree, the answer lies in the momentum generated by specific issues. In the United States, in particular, the campaign for civil rights had an enormous impact in radicalizing student opinion.

## The Elements of Protest

As formulated by its leader, Martin Luther King, in the late 1950s and early 1960s, the civil rights campaign was not a challenge to the American way of life. It was rather a demand that the United States live up to its

Che Guevara, pictured here in the early 1950s, was adopted as an icon by many disaffected young people and became a favorite subject for posters in student rooms.

principles of freedom and democracy by guaranteeing rights to African Americans in the white-dominated southern states. Students, both black and white, were in the forefront of this movement, braving violent prejudice with sit-ins at segregated lunch counters and freedom rides that challenged segregation in travel facilities. Gradually, the hostility they often encountered led young civil rights activists to question the whole nature of American society.

Another major focus of 1960s protest was opposition to war. Europeans protested against the proliferation of nuclear weapons, for example. When the conflict in which the United States was involved in Vietnam (*see 8:1100*) escalated from the mid-1960s onward, antiwar sentiment guaranteed that the response among many young people would be hostile. The Vietnam War did more than any other single issue to fuel student protest, both in the United States and in Europe.

Many young people came to feel that the United States was not really the land of democracy, freedom, and equal opportu-

1163

véritable

C G

French students and sympathizers from the labor unions march in Paris in May 1968. The students' protests were violently put down by French police.

nity but a land of exploitation, racism, and violent oppression that showed its true face in the South and in Vietnam. Students for a Democratic Society (SDS), one of the more extreme left-wing groups in America, asked in 1965: "What kind of an America is it whose response to poverty and oppression in Vietnam is napalm and defoliation? Whose response to poverty and oppression in Mississippi is silence?"

### Radical Ideas

To respond to what they saw as a society in crisis, people adopted radical forms of thinking, a major strand of which was anti-authoritarianism. Young radicals wanted an end to what the German student leader Rudi Dutschke called "the power of people over people." They argued that a democracy that consisted of voting for one of two or three almost identical candidates every

few years was no democracy at all and that people's lives were in fact controlled by governments, bureaucracies, and corporations over which they had no control. The radicals demanded "participatory democracy," with which people would take direct control of their workplace, campus, or community.

Another strand of protest focused on the developing world. Radical thinkers were reinterpreting the history of Western society not as a story of inexorable progress but as a process of enslavement and extermination. American author Susan Sontag wrote in 1966, "The white race is the cancer of human history." One of the most popular icons of the period was Ernesto "Che" Guevara, an Argentinian-born colleague of Cuba's Fidel Castro. Guevara dreamed of leading a worldwide revolt by the poor of the earth against "Western imperialism."

Communist leaders Ho Chi Minh of North Vietnam and Mao Tse-tung of China also appealed to many Western student radicals, by whom they were adopted as symbols of the developing world's revolt against Western oppression.

More directly based in the everyday experience of young people in the 1960s was a demand for the freedom to pursue sexual experimentation and explore new lifestyles. This was given forthright expression in 1964 by German-born U.S. professor Herbert Marcuse in his *One-Dimensional Man*. Marcuse saw Western society as being characterized by "repressive tolerance" in which genuine human satisfaction was forbidden. In its place, people were given the illusion of fulfilment through the ownership of consumer goods.

In 1968, the tide of antiauthoritarian and revolutionary feeling among students reached its peak, causing upheavals and disturbances in many countries. In the United States, students occupied Columbia University, New York City, in April 1968, and antiwar protests at the Chicago Democratic Convention in August ended with fighting between demonstrators and police. West Germany and Italy also experienced major disturbances. France, however, experienced the nearest thing to a genuine revolution.

The brutal police repression of student protests in May 1968 brought French workers out on strike in support of the students. A wave of occupations of workplaces swept the country. Factory workers took over their factories, bank clerks their banks, and shopworkers department stores. For a month, French economic life came to a halt. The students' worker allies were eventually bought off with large pay raises, while national elections revealed that the revolutionaries had less popular support than expected.

The student revolts of the late 1960s failed to achieve the radical social transformation they desired. Some of the would-be revolutionaries refused to renounce their vision of the imminent downfall of consumer society and subsequently turned to terrorist violence. Groups such as the Baader-Meinhof Gang in West Germany, the Red Brigades in Italy, and, to a lesser degree, the Weathermen in the United States, waged a futile war on the authorities with bombs and guns in the 1970s.

## Liberation

There were many positive results of the agitation of the 1960s. One was the growth of a powerful popular environmental

Marchers pass demolished buildings in Washington, D.C., to demonstrate for welfare rights as part of a so-called Poor People's Campaign in 1968.

A sticker produced by the U.S. gay organization Stonewall proclaims the group's aim, equal rights for homosexuals by the year 2000.

1165

movement campaigning against pollution, the exhaustion of natural resources, and the destruction of animal and plant species (*see 9:1263*). Many of the "green" campaigners of the 1970s were former 1960s' student activists. The example of the civil rights movement also led to a demand for full rights from other groups who saw themselves as victims of prejudice and disadvantage, including Hispanics and Native Americans in the United States. From 1969, homosexuals campaigned effectively against discrimination through the gay liberation movement.

The most powerful example of "rights politics," however, was the women's movement. The new wave of feminism is normally traced to the publication of Betty Friedan's book *The Feminine Mystique* in 1963, which attacked the notion that American women should be satisfied with the domestic roles of wife and mother. In 1966, Friedan and others founded the

National Organization for Women, or NOW, which specifically placed its claim for equality for American women in the context of "the worldwide revolution of human rights now taking place within and beyond our national borders." In the early 1970s, the movement for women's liberation gathered large-scale support in the United States and many West European countries. The United Nations declared 1975 the first International Women's Year.

American feminists saw one of their most important demands met in 1973 when the Supreme Court ruled that a woman had the right to choose to have an abortion. This was one of a series of decisions by the Supreme Court in the 1960s and 1970s that brought controversial changes to American society, including the effective suspension of capital punishment and legalization of pornography. Similar changes in western Europe differed from country to country. In Britain, for example, the Labour government of 1964 to 1970 legalized abortion, made divorce easier to obtain, decriminalized homosexual acts between consenting adults, and abolished capital punishment. Catholic states in Europe still ruled abortion and homosexuality illegal, however.

## The 1970s: A Political Turning Point

In the United States, the reaction against liberal legislation and radical agitation can be traced back at least as far as the election of a conservative Republican, ex-movie star Ronald Reagan, as governor of California in 1966. Two years later, Richard Nixon's victory in the 1968 presidential elections confirmed the beginning of the right-wing backlash. In the wider world, however, liberals, socialists, and communists held the political initiative into the mid-1970s. The U.S. policy of détente with communist China and the Soviet Union in the early 1970s in practice amounted to an acceptance of the legitimacy of communist rule over much of the world. In 1975, the United States was humiliated by the triumph of communist forces in Vietnam, Cambodia, and Laos.

In western Europe, the Italian Communist Party launched a new bid for popular support by embracing what was called Eurocommunism. Eurocommunism differed from Marxist communism in its respect for political freedom and the free market. The Italian communists' election performance brought them close to a share of political power. In Portugal, a military coup in 1974 brought left-wing army officers to power. In West Germany, the Social Democratic Party held power throughout

A woman in Denver, Colorado, shows her support for speakers during a pro-abortion rights rally in November 1989. Women's right to an abortion was the subject of one of the most heated political debates of the 1980s and 1990s.

the 1970s. In Britain, strike action by militant trade unionists brought down the Conservative government of the early 1970s, and a Labour government with a left-wing program was elected in 1974.

From the mid-1970s, however, the balance of the political debate began to shift. Communism once more revealed a harsh face when the Marxist triumphs in Cambodia and Vietnam were followed by massacres and misgovernment that led to the death or flight into exile of millions of people. The Soviet invasion of Afghanistan at the end of 1979 provided further ammunition for anticommunist publicists. Meanwhile, the people who had argued that the "permissive" liberal legislation of the 1960s would undermine Western society pointed to sharply rising crime rates and divorce and illegitimacy figures as evidence that they had been right.

The single most crucial development of the 1970s, however, was the end of the postwar economic boom in the United States and Western Europe. By 1974, rapid economic growth and rising prosperity had been replaced by rising inflation and mass unemployment. Milton Friedman, professor of economics at Chicago University and winner of the 1976 Nobel Prize for Economics, argued that the interventionist policies of Western governments were to

blame for the economic downturn. In a return to the theory that had held sway before the 1930s, he argued that the state should not try to manage or control the economy. The sole function of the state was to maintain an appropriate money supply, balance its budget, and allow an unrestricted market and unlimited competition. This would produce a maximum of goods, services, and human happiness.

Friedman's views became immensely influential in the 1980s. With the election of Margaret Thatcher as British prime minister in 1979 and then of Ronald Reagan as U.S. president in the fall of 1980, a decisive swing to the right had taken place. Although there were again considerable variations from country to country, during the 1980s and 1990s the governments of North America and western Europe in general became committed to cuts in taxation, deregulation of the economy, reductions in welfare spending, balanced budgets, and the privatization of nationalized industries. Both the mixed economy and the welfare state were either abandoned or put on the defensive. The commitment to maintaining full employment was dropped.

These policies were accompanied, at least in Britain and the United States, by attempts to reassert what people claimed were traditional morality and family values.

Margaret Thatcher, Britain's first female prime minister, led the country from 1979 to 1990. Together with her ally and friend Ronald Reagan, Thatcher was highly influential in shaping Western conservatism in the 1980s.

London's Telecom Tower was adopted by the British government as an effective symbol of the privatization of nationalized industries, particularly the telephone industry, in the mid-1980s.

The United States resumed capital punishment from 1977 and gradually introduced stricter sentencing policies that produced a sharp rise in prison populations. Policies of affirmative action, designed to achieve racial equality through setting quotas for African American employment and education, came under attack. Many of the rights achieved by women, blacks, gays, and other groups were maintained, however. There was no possibility of a return to the restrictive laws of the pre-1960s.

### The Postcommunist World

The West's swing to the right at the start of the 1980s was accompanied by strongly anticommunist views. Ronald Reagan famously referred to the Soviet Union as the "evil empire." After the emergence of Mikhail Gorbachev as a reforming Soviet leader in 1985, however, communism collapsed (*see 9:1243*) in eastern Europe and then in the Soviet Union itself. In East Asia, China, the other bastion of communism, adopted many aspects of a free-enterprise, free-market economy (*see 9:1186*).

The triumph of liberal democracy by the 1990s was remarkable. Most of Eastern Europe and the former Soviet Union now had elected governments that respected basic freedoms. In western Europe, Greece, Spain, and Portugal had been ruled by authoritarian governments until the mid-1970s but had become democracies. In South and Central America, where the United States backed numerous military regimes up to the 1980s, governments evolved in the direction of democratic civilian rule. Although there were still many regimes that abused human rights and denied fundamental freedoms, such as Iraq and China, there was no longer a coherent political ideology arguing against the liberal democratic ideal.

The triumph of global capitalism was even more complete. It seemed to be almost universally acknowledged that the best way to create wealth was to allow more or less free enterprise to flourish. Giant multinational companies operated on a world scale, setting up factories wherever they could find cheap labor and shifting capital from country to country.

The world still faced many problems (*see 9:1273*). These ranged from the failure of unregulated capitalism to produce prosperity in the former Soviet Union to the persistence of warfare in parts of the world and the ongoing ecological crisis created by the growth of human population and consumption. Such issues would fuel fresh political debates into the new millennium.

# Life in the Nuclear Age

*The Changing Face of America*

The end of World War II confirmed the United States as the most powerful nation on earth. While European countries faced the enormous problem of postwar redevelopment (*see 8:1071*), America went from strength to strength. In the 1950s, the booming American economy and the country's political dominance brought the realization of the so-called American dream for the white middle class. Anyone prepared to work hard in America's free and democratic society, the vision promised, could achieve financial and social success. The same potent message surfaced in other periods of the late twentieth century, such as during the presidency of Bill Clinton. Not even the specter of the "witch-hunts"

staged by Senator Joe McCarthy from 1950 to 1954 to root out perceived communists in American life affected the United States' buoyant optimism.

## Booming Economy

The 1950s were a period of unprecedented growth that was unimaginable to those who had experienced the Great Depression. National output doubled: America was responsible for two-thirds of the world's industrial production. In mid-1949 the average per capita income of an American citizen was $1,450; in western Europe, the equivalent figure was about half that amount. Over the next decade, personal incomes tripled, and America's affluent

An advertisement from the late 1950s captures the essential elements of the American dream: a perfect middle-class family, a comfortable home, and plenty to eat.

Cottage Grove, southwest of St. Paul, Minnesota, typifies the suburban housing that became popular in the 1950s. With new tract housing, the town's population grew in the mid-1950s from 883 to nearly 5,000.

A 1953 Buick Skylark. High incomes made car ownership common in the United States, and manufacturers constantly introduced new features and models to corner a share of the lucrative but highly competitive market.

ters for the suburbs, where they could fulfill their dream of owning a modern house and garden. In just four years, Levitt built 17,447 houses on 6,000 acres of land outside Hempstead, New York. The neighborhood, known as Levittown, became the blueprint for thousands of suburban developments that sprang up all over America. Levitt's dream did not include everyone. He laid down strict conditions about who could live in his houses: black Americans were not allowed.

### The Rise in Consumerism
Accompanying the housing boom was a rapid rise in consumerism. The number of families owning two cars doubled between 1951 and 1958. Most men went out to work while the majority of women stayed at home, raising children and looking after domestic matters. Many housewives, particularly middle-class women, found themselves isolated in their new homes, having perhaps moved to a new state because of their husband's job. Women's days were often defined by boredom. New labor-saving gadgets did away with many traditional daily chores while at the same time introducing new ones. Radio and television showed a stream of advertisements that put pressure on women to conform to new stereotypes of ideal wives and mothers. Where their grandmother might have taken rugs outside a few times a year to beat them clean, for example, 1950s women were advised to use a vacuum cleaner daily on their new wall-to-wall carpet.

middle class expanded to include around 60 percent of the population.

As salaries increased so did disposable incomes. Americans went on a spending spree, and their chief purchase was often real estate. A housing boom between 1948 and 1958 produced thirteen million new homes. The builder Bill Levitt helped change the face of the nation. Levitt constructed middle-class houses cheaply and quickly and equipped them with the latest domestic features that modern technology could produce, such as central heating, refrigerators, and washing machines. Levitt offered to build houses for World War II veterans that not only were cheap but required no down payment. He was besieged. A rising birthrate fueled the need for new homes. Newly prosperous Americans were eager to leave urban cen-

### Popular Culture
Two defining elements of everyday life in the 1950s were television and music. Television had quickly supplanted radio's role as America's chief source of home

entertainment. By the mid-1950s, some 83 percent of American households owned a television set. The Korean War (1950–1953) became the first "media" war, although it was not until the war in Vietnam over a decade later that television news programs transmitted graphic war reports. By then, TV had become a highly influential shaper of public attitudes toward the conflict. In the 1950s, popular TV shows included formulaic situation comedies, such as *I Love Lucy,* that became a permanent cultural reference.

In music, the beginning of the decade saw the emergence of rock and roll and the rise of performers such as Bill Haley (1925–1981), Elvis Presley (1935–1977), and Chuck Berry (b. 1926). Rock and roll brought together influences from rhythm and blues, country music, and even gospel to create a young, distinctly American music that crossed color boundaries. Until the 1950s, rhythm and blues, like jazz before it, had been the music mainly of black musicians. Elvis Presley and other performers inspired generations of bands and singers on both sides of the Atlantic.

The emergence of rock and roll was a testament to the new influence of young people in America. Teenagers frequently earned money from Saturday jobs that they could spend on records, clothes, or entertainment. They spent their time in their cars at drive-ins listening to rock music or went to drive-in movies. While glamour-starved, postwar European moviegoers flocked to 1940s Hollywood movies, American audiences preferred a different type of film. The movies that talked to the rock and roll generation displayed the disaffection of the young and the growing generation gap. No star captured the disaffection better than James Dean (1931–1955) in the movie *Rebel Without A Cause* (1955). Dean personified contemporary American youth's sense of restlessness and lack of purpose. In literature, the "beat generation" of writers, led by Jack Kerouac (1922–1969), author of *On the Road* (1957), described an aimless, structureless life. Kerouac's America was the antithesis of the idealized suburban lifestyle.

### The Rise in Black Activism
America in the 1950s was full of contradictions. Material life had never been better, but rising living standards encouraged increased expectations that could not be satisfied for millions of Americans on low incomes with few prospects. Particularly excluded were African American citizens. Since the end of World War II, African

Dubbed "Elvis the Pelvis," Elvis Presley, pictured in the late 1950s, became an icon of youthful revolt when he scandalized older Americans with his hip-swinging dancing.

Americans, particularly veterans who had fought for the United States, had grown less willing to accept the segregation and discrimination they experienced on a daily basis. Millions of black Americans left the South in the 1940s and 1950s in search of a better life. There were sporadic acts of defiance against segregation, however, such as Rosa Parks's refusal to give up her bus seat to a white man in Montgomery, Alabama, in 1955. Parks's action sparked a yearlong bus boycott by the local black population. As the decade progressed, such acts became increasingly well coordinated and effective. They were the forerunners of the civil rights movement of the 1960s.

### The 1960s
By the end of the 1950s, cracks were appearing within American society as the greater expectations fostered by the economic boom gave way to the discontent and disillusion that largely characterized the 1960s in the United States. People living through the decade were aware that they were witnessing fundamental changes in society. Bob Dylan sang in 1964, "the times they are a-changin'." The American dream was growing increasingly tarnished.

This early foil packet of contraceptive pills represented sexual freedom for millions of women.

Martin Luther King, in the black gown, addresses the crowd at the Lincoln Memorial in Washington, D.C., during his "I Have a Dream" speech in August 1963.

Some people believe that the American dream died with the assassination of President John F. Kennedy on November 22, 1963 (*see 9:1173*). Others contend that U.S. involvement in Vietnam spelled the end of the public's admiration for its gov-

ernment (*see 8:1100*). Whenever the change began, the decade came to epitomize radical social and political change and a complex relationship between prosperity and achievement on one hand and discontent on the other. In 1969, U.S. technology put an astronaut on the moon. That same year, protests against the Vietnam War swept university campuses, and state troopers marched in American streets.

## Equal Rights for Women

In 1960, the contraceptive pill was licensed for sale, providing women with a reliable and accessible means to avoid pregnancy. The freedom brought by the pill provoked a sexual revolution, coinciding as it did with women's increasing frustration at their limited roles as wives and mothers. Divorce rates, which had been very low between 1947 and 1963, began to rise in the early 1960s and then skyrocketed in the 1970s and 1980s, when 50 percent of marriages ended in divorce.

*The Feminine Mystique* (1963), written by Betty Friedan (b. 1921), was an influen-

# The Death of Camelot

For many people, the moment the American dream died is easy to specify. It was 12:30 P.M. CST on Friday, November 22, 1963. That was the moment two rifle bullets struck President John F. Kennedy in the neck and the head as he drove in a motorcade through downtown Dallas. Just over two hours later, at 2:38 P.M., Vice President Lyndon B. Johnson was sworn in as president on board Air Force One. An era was over.

Such is the myth that grew up around John Fitzgerald Kennedy that it is sometimes difficult to remember that his presidency only lasted 1,037 days, or a little under three years. The shock that greeted Kennedy's assassination, however, was the result not so much of what the president had achieved but of what he promised and what he symbolized.

Kennedy, a World War II hero from a Massachusetts Irish-American political dynasty, was good looking and talented, glamorous and charming. The youngest man ever to be elected president, Kennedy embodied the optimism of the United States at the start of the 1960s. "We stand on the edge of a new frontier," he claimed in his acceptance speech as Democratic presidential candidate. At his inauguration he announced his commitment to defending freedom around the world and called on Americans "to bear the burden of a long twilight struggle... against the common enemies of man: tyranny, poverty, disease, and war itself." Such was the self-confidence of the United States that Americans eagerly embraced a view of themselves as the world's defenders of democracy.

As president, Kennedy attracted a circle of young and gifted advisers. Some observers likened the administration to the court of the legendary King Arthur, Camelot, the home of the Knights of the Round Table. Among Kennedy's leading courtiers were his wife, Jacqueline Bouvier Kennedy (1929–1994), and his younger brother, Robert F. Kennedy, who served as attorney general.

The image of Kennedy's Camelot as a symbol of promise proved enduring, despite subsequent scandals about his personal life. Kennedy's idealistic rhetoric was also undermined by foreign affairs disasters such as the abortive invasion of communist Cuba at the Bay of Pigs in

April 1961 (*see 8:1096*). That the romantic image of Kennedy's administration survives perhaps owes much to the violent tragedy in which it ended.

The Kennedy assassination shocked the world, but the dignified conduct of his family in its aftermath did much to raise the Kennedy mystique. Jacqueline Kennedy became almost revered, even after she married Greek shipping magnate Aristotle Onassis in 1968. That same year, Robert Kennedy was assassinated as he campaigned for the presidency.

Lee Harvey Oswald was arrested for the assassination of John F. Kennedy and was himself gunned down two days later. Rumors persist that Oswald was part of a conspiracy involving the Mafia, communist sympathizers, and even the CIA itself. The 1964 Warren Commission, however, determined that the murder was committed by Oswald alone.

Three-year-old John Kennedy salutes at his father's funeral on November 25, 1963. The front row of mourners, from left to right, includes Senator Edward Kennedy, Caroline Kennedy, Jacqueline Kennedy and Attorney General Robert Kennedy.

President Lyndon B. Johnson addresses U.S. senators and political leaders in the White House during the signing of the Civil Rights Bill on July 2, 1964.

Soldiers take cover behind a police car during race riots in Newark, New Jersey, in 1967. They are trying to locate the position of a sniper firing from a window opposite.

tial articulation of women's frustrations and helped inspire the American women's liberation movement. Women fought for the right to equal opportunity and equal pay with men. Quotas restricted the number of women who could enter professions such as engineering, law, and medicine. At the end of the 1960s, women earned little more than half as much as men. Women protested throughout the 1960s, and in 1972, they eventually succeeded in winning equal opportunities with men, at least on paper.

## The Civil Rights Movement

Perhaps the most important social phenomenon of the 1960s, or even of the century, was the civil rights movement. The movement sought to give black Americans equal rights with their white compatriots. The oppression and bigotry experienced by African Americans in every aspect of life, particularly in the South, segregated society as completely as the apartheid system did in South Africa (*see 9:1228*).

The civil rights movement brought to prominence a generation of outstanding African American leaders, including Malcolm X (1925–1965) and Jesse Jackson (b. 1941). The most famous activist, however, was Martin Luther King (1929–1968), a Baptist minister who came to national attention during the Alabama bus boycott. King addressed the crowd at the end of the first black march on Washington, D.C., in May 1957, calling for an end to voting restrictions. The speech established him as the leader of the civil rights movement. King's campaign of nonviolence was influenced by the tactics of the Indian independence leader Mahatma Gandhi (*see 8:1108*). King's sit-ins, marches, and attempts to register to vote provoked various responses from white Americans.

An inspirational orator, King made many important speeches. One of the most famous came at the end of a 200,000-person march on Washington, D.C., on August 23, 1963. Repeating the phrase "I have a dream," King spoke passionately about a future America in which blacks and whites would live equally. Shortly afterward, four black girls attending Sunday school were killed in the bombing of a church in Birmingham, Alabama.

After nearly a decade, the civil rights movement finally brought legislative change. President Lyndon B. Johnson (1908–1973), Kennedy's successor, argued that continued racism could only be divisive and damaging to the United States. On July 2, 1964, Johnson signed the Civil Rights Act, banning discrimination in public services and employment. In 1965, Congress struck down many state's restrictions on black Americans' right to vote.

## The Great Society

In pursuit of what he termed the Great Society, Johnson introduced the greatest mass of social legislation since the New Deal of the 1930s. New laws affected education, legal aid, job training, urban renewal, and health care. Social unrest continued, however, and the National Guard became a regular sight on the streets of the nation's cities. Serious race riots broke out in the Watts section of Los Angeles in August 1965 and in Newark, New Jersey, and Detroit in July 1967. In Detroit, unrest sparked by resentment of the nearly all-white police force left 43 people dead, more than 1,000 injured, 7,000 under arrest, and 5,000 homeless.

## The Generation Gap

Society's apparent racism was a source of profound disillusionment for many young Americans. Escalating U.S. involvement in the Vietnam War was another. Some young people saw the United States as little freer than the Soviet Union it opposed in the Cold War. Society's real enemies, they believed, were not communists, but the traditional elite and vested interests who oppressed individual rights and led the United States into needless conflict.

A flyer from 1967 advertises a concert by seminal hippie band Jefferson Airplane. Such bands epitomized youth rebellion against the U.S. establishment.

1175

Crowds at the Woodstock rock festival in August 1969. The festival, which attracted around 450,000 young people, marked the high point of America's counterculture in the 1960s.

By the late 1960s, many young people consciously rejected all traditional values. They turned their backs on the American dream that had inspired their parents. Young women rejected a life in which they were expected to find contentment through housework and caring for a family. Many young men abandoned the role in which they returned from work to spend the evening in slippers in front of the television.

The idea of the nuclear family itself was under threat. Some of the young rejected marriage as restrictive, particularly in the role it imposed on women. The contraceptive pill encouraged sexual freedom. In a few areas, communes became popular, places where adults and their children joined to live in small communities based upon the equitable distribution of labor.

### The Counterculture

Young people rejected even the appearance of their elders. Many grew their hair long and wore distinctive clothes, which often incorporated elements of costume from the developing world. Another manifestation of the growing divide between young and old came in the youth culture's liberal attitude toward music and drugs, epitomized in the free rock concert at Woodstock, in upstate New York, in August 1969.

The attitudes of hippies and other youth movements were not entirely prompted by a rejection of the past. Some reflected idealistic optimism for the future. The young really did hope that wars could be avoided, society made more equal, and racism defeated, so long as power lay with individuals rather than governments or other forms of authority. Some members of the establishment, particularly academics, endorsed the youth counterculture. They believed that it encouraged people to expand their perception and to question traditional values.

### The 1970s

Late in the 1960s, a series of events further shocked the people of the United States. In 1968, Martin Luther King and Robert Kennedy both fell victim to assassins. On May 4, 1970, four students died when National Guardsmen fired on anti-Vietnam protesters at Kent State University, Ohio. The deaths prompted 400 campuses to shut down. More than two million students went on strike. In the furor, the killing of two black students at Jackson State College by Mississippi state police was almost entirely overlooked.

In 1972, a break-in at the Democratic Party headquarters at Washington's Water-

Evangelist Billy Graham shakes hands with admirers in a photograph taken in 1966. Graham was highly influential in born-again Christianity and acted as spiritual adviser to Lyndon Johnson.

gate Hotel led to revelations of illegal practices and financial irregularities that implicated top Republican officials. The scandal culminated in 1974 in the resignation of President Richard Nixon (1913–1994), shortly before impeachment proceedings began against him.

The decline in public confidence in government was exacerbated by recession. Between 1947 and 1973, incomes had risen annually by an average of 2.7 percent. In the 1970s, incomes began a fall that continued into the early 1980s. Families relied on both parents working full-time to maintain their standard of living. In 1940, only 26 percent of women worked; by 1970, the figure was 42 percent and was rising.

Women both needed and wanted to work. Sexual freedom was extended in 1973 to the right of abortion. Women had more control over their bodies than they had ever known. They used their freedom to make great strides in the professions and continued their fight for equal rights.

## Disillusion with Government

It was no longer only the young who questioned the government's suitability to govern. People on the Right saw the movement for women's equality as a symptom of moral collapse, along with other movements, such as the fight for gay rights, which gathered momentum throughout the 1970s. The Left, meanwhile, saw Vietnam and Watergate as proof of America's loss of leadership. In both cases, liberal sympathizers believed, the administration had systematically deceived the American people. Failure in Vietnam, moreover, ended Americans' belief in their nation's omnipotence and the liberal consensus that the United States had a duty to fight for freedom anywhere in the world.

By the end of the 1970s, the middle-class, far from living the American dream, was worried about job security, inflation, crime, permissiveness, and race relations. One response to the moral vacuum in public life was the rightist rhetoric of Ronald Reagan (b. 1911), who became president in 1981. Another came from a Christian organization in the South, the Moral Majority.

Dwarfed by a huge flag, President Richard Nixon makes a speech in November 1973. The next year, Nixon resigned when it became clear that he had tried to cover up his role in the Watergate scandal.

A scene from *The Cosby Show* from 1985 shows Bill Cosby with his TV wife played Phylicia Ayers-Allen (later Phylicia Rashad). The popular comedy portrayed the lives of a well-off black middle-class family. Offscreen, Cosby became for a time the highest paid entertainer in the United States.

## The Moral Majority

The largely Protestant moral majority emerged in the southern states ostensibly to combat a moral decline in America's schools by urging a fundamentalist, literal understanding of the Bible and of Christian morality. The organization worked to get Reagan's Republicans elected in 1980, seeing the political right as the best answer to problems such as drugs, prostitution, violent crime, and pornography. While mainstream church membership fell by several million between 1965 and 1980, membership of the Southern Baptist Church rose from 10.8 to 13.6 million. Among the leaders of the Southern Baptist Church was the charismatic and influential preacher Billy Graham (b. 1918).

Many of the new ministries in the South promoted born-again Christianity, which encouraged adults to reaffirm their commitment to their faith. Their beliefs were often attacked as antigay, anti-Semitic, antiwomen, anti-Catholic, and antiurban. The churches embraced television, and there was a rise in conservative and evangelical TV preachers, such as Jim Bakker. In 1978, twenty-five Christian ministries were broadcasting; by 1989, the number was 336. Some churches were later found guilty of corruption. Jim Bakker was jailed for fraud and conspiracy after his mistress reported his business dealings.

## The Rise of Economic Disparity

The policies of the Reagan administration failed to lessen a growing division in American life, where society was more divided between rich and poor than ever before. The contrast was most marked in the cities. In New York City's Harlem, significant numbers of children dealt in crack cocaine; downtown, in trendy SoHo, a new breed of monied, young, urban professionals, dubbed yuppies, bought cocaine for recreation. The yuppies were a characteristic product of the 1980s. Often working in banking, the law, and the media, they were extremely well paid and, aided by tax cuts introduced by Reagan, had surplus money to spend.

## The Emergence of a Black Middle Class

Johnson's introduction of the Immigration Reform Act in 1965 changed the ethnic mix of the United States. Eighty-five percent of the more than sixteen million immigrants who entered the United States between 1968 and 1992 came from the developing world, with 47 percent from Latin America alone. African Americans, who traditionally had poorer-paying jobs than their white peers, competed for low-paid work with the new immigrants.

In the 1960s, affirmative action had introduced quotas in employment and education that discriminated in favor of minorities, particularly African Americans and women. Black Americans were able to train and work in fields that were previously closed to them. By the time affirmative action came under criticism in the 1980s, a new professional black middle class had emerged. Only three decades after the Civil Rights Act, the number of black families with an income above $50,000 had quadrupled. Atlanta, Georgia, and other cities had large black middle-class populations enjoying their own share of the American dream.

# China: 1949–1999

## The Communists in Power

Writing in the mid–nineteenth century, Karl Marx, the founder of communism, predicted that revolutions would arise in industrial societies where workers lived in miserable conditions in towns and cities. These workers would inevitably rise up against the capitalists who profited from their labor (*see 6:812*).

Marx's prediction of the nature of revolution has been proved wrong many times, among them in China in 1949. There, Mao Tse-tung and his communists came to power with the support of millions of peasant farmers rather than urban workers. China was industrially so underdeveloped that, according to Marx's theory, it should not have been ready for communist revolution. The same was true of Vietnam in the 1950s and Cuba in 1958 (*see 8:1096*). As in China, communists came to power in these countries for reasons that Marx did

not predict: to get rid of long-term poverty, hated foreign domination, and the old, corrupt ruling classes.

### Mao's Daunting Undertaking

One reason Mao won so many followers was that he promised to deliver China from the poverty that had dominated life for most people for centuries. Having defeated the nationalists of Chiang Kai-shek after years of warfare, Mao had to turn to the difficult task of fulfilling this promise (*see 7:936*).

Unlike revolutionaries who have seized power elsewhere, the Chinese communists had considerable experience of governing: since the early 1930s, they had controlled large parts of the country. Even so, the tasks that lay ahead were daunting. For one thing, the communists faced a hostile world. Western governments refused to

A member of China's Red Army examines a stereo at an electronics store in Shanghai in this photograph from 1985. China's history since the death of Mao Tse-tung in 1976 has involved establishing a balance between communist idealism and capitalist economic progress.

A communist prepares to execute a landowner in 1949 in the aftermath of the Chinese Revolution.

recognize the new regime in Beijing and continued to support Chiang Kai-shek, who had set up a government in exile on the off-shore island of Taiwan. The Soviet Union was the only country of any size and importance to give official support to the new China. In February 1950, Mao visited Soviet leader Joseph Stalin in Moscow, where the two communist governments signed a treaty of friendship. The Soviet Union agreed to lend a large sum of money to China, and to provide it with technical assistance in a variety of areas.

China was in dire need of such help. Even compared to India, another large, undeveloped Asian country, its economy was extremely backward. India produced twice as much electricity, for instance, and had three times as many miles of railroad track. In every sector of industry, China was less productive than Russia had been on the eve of World War I. Mao knew that he needed to industrialize his country and that this would be a huge undertaking. He therefore devoted himself first to more immediate reforms to win the good will of the wider population.

Mao's government first tackled corruption, successfully getting rid of bandits and crooked local officials. In the countryside,

land was taken away from big landowners and given out to peasants in small plots of about 2.5 acres. By 1952, grain production had reached record levels. The railroad system, battered by years of warfare, was repaired and extended. Inflation was brought down and a fairer tax system introduced. Food and clothing were distributed to many people in need.

By the end of 1952, great progress had been made in a number of areas, though not everyone yet accepted the full authority of the communists. As a result, the government launched campaigns of "thought reform" to bring opponents of one-party communist rule into line. Those people who refused to be "reeducated"—especially landowners and businessmen—were simply executed. Between 1949 and 1952, more than one million opponents of the regime were put to death.

## Industrial and Military Growth

In 1953, Mao followed the example set by the Soviet Union in the late 1920s by introducing the first five-year plan for industry. The state seized control of almost all privately owned industrial companies and directed investment toward heavy industry, especially the production of iron

Photographed in 1967, workers gather hay on a communal farm.

and steel. Large amounts of money were also spent on strengthening the country's defenses and its armed forces.

As the Cold War intensified between the Soviet Union and the West (*see 8:1092*), China found itself caught in the middle with few friends. Chinese leaders also felt threatened by American demands for Chiang Kai-shek and the nationalists to be restored to power on the mainland. To make matters worse, China suffered from its involvement in the Korean War from November 1950. Chinese troops helped North Korea push back United Nations forces as they approached the Chinese frontier. Chinese armies were decisive in

Families of a farm collective enjoy lunch in this photograph from the early 1960s. Rice was provided free by the collective, but there was a small charge for meat and vegetables to accompany it.

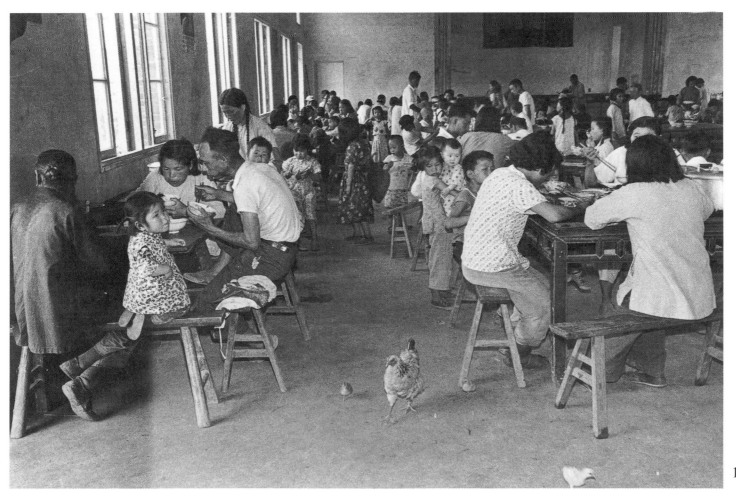

Tanks parade through Beijing's Tiananmen Square in 1959. China's tense relations with its neighbors—especially India and, from 1956, the Soviet Union—made it important to maintain a strong military capability.

saving the North Koreans from defeat but at the cost of more than one million dead. More important, perhaps, the war defined China as an enemy of the West, a position it would hold for decades.

**Agricultural Restructuring**

After initially handing out small farms to peasants, Mao decided to follow the Soviet example and force the same peasants onto large collective farms. Private ownership of land, except for small garden plots, was officially abolished. By 1957, all peasants had been enrolled in collective farms. Profits were shared among all the members of a collective, according to how many hours they worked on the farm and the value of the tools they used.

In the Soviet Union, this policy had been disastrous, resulting in widespread famine and protests that the government suppressed; millions died of hunger or in the crackdown that followed (*see 7:922*). China was more fortunate: its experiment with collectivization had better results. Those who still protested the system were "reeducated" or executed.

At this point, the protests of peasant farmers were of little concern to Chinese leaders. What troubled them more was opposition from educated Chinese, dubbed intellectuals; living in towns and cities. In an important speech to Communist Party

leaders in May 1956, Mao declared that the time had come for the party to listen to useful criticism of what it was doing. "Let a hundred flowers bloom," he announced. "Let a hundred schools contend."

In effect, Mao was saying that he and his government welcomed freedom of speech. Yet he seemed startled by the torrent of criticism that followed. People questioned the dictatorial methods of the Communist Party, and some even attacked Mao himself. Before a year was out, the communists had learned to look upon these criticisms not as flowers but as poisonous weeds. In the spring of 1957, the government turned on its critics, imprisoning many thousands of intellectuals and removing 200,000 of them from towns to the countryside to be reeducated in the virtues of communism. Some people believe that Mao's hundred flowers speech was a sham staged to trick the communists' enemies into the open. Other people believe the initiative was a genuine attempt to build bridges between the party and Chinese intellectuals that simply backfired.

**The Great Leap Forward**

There followed the disaster of the Great Leap Forward, as Mao called his grand program to make China catch up with the West. Although the Chinese economy was growing faster than ever before, it was still

Although collective farming barely provided enough food for some Chinese peasants, such as this couple, China still exported grain to countries as far away as Albania.

losing ground to the economies of the West during the boom years of the 1950s. In 1958, Mao therefore set fresh production targets to increase output for both industry and agriculture. The targets were unrealistic, but everyone was forced to try to meet them. Some factories banned meal breaks and created long shifts to keep operating for twenty-four hours a day. In the countryside, farms were turned into inefficient "factories," many of which were dedicated to making steel. These were little more than backyard furnaces, consuming vital raw materials and producing steel of such a low grade that it could not be used.

It rapidly became apparent that the Great Leap Forward was bound to fail. Within a year of its introduction in 1958, Mao himself acknowledged his role in the failure when he resigned as head of the central government council, though he remained chairman of the Communist Party.

The scale of the economic catastrophe grew. The consequences of trying to turn farms into factories produced such poor harvests from 1959 to 1961 that China plunged into famine. Communist officials continued to proclaim that targets were being met and that there were no food shortages, but in some parts of the country, people were so desperate that they resorted to cannibalism. It is estimated that up to thirty million people starved to death in those three years alone.

The cost in human lives was made worse by the failure of the Great Leap Forward to achieve even its most basic aims. Not only did Chinese industries fail to meet their new targets, their output actually declined sharply. The progress that had been made since 1949 was undone at a stroke.

## Liu's Rule

Mao's successor as head of the central council was Liu Shao-chi (1898–1969), a great organizer who had opposed the Great Leap Forward. Liu now turned the clock back, allowing peasants to regain their private plots. Farms were returned to farming, while factory workers were given prizes and bonuses to encourage production. For his efforts, Liu would later be denounced during the Cultural Revolution as China's "number one capitalist roader," meaning that he was leading China back along the road to capitalism. He was removed from his position in 1968 and disappeared from public life, dying in obscurity in 1974.

In his semiretirement, Mao grew angry at the prospect of a return to social inequality and private industry. In 1962, Liu's impli-

This statue of Chairman Mao stands in the city of Kashgar in Xinjiang province. The efforts of the Red Guards gave Mao's personality cult an almost religious status.

1183

# The Cultural Revolution

In August 1966, Mao Tse-tung launched the Great Proletarian Cultural Revolution. In Mao's view, the hostility between China and the Soviet Union showed that the Russian Revolution had lost its way; he was also concerned about his own diminished role in China's revolution. The Cultural Revolution aimed to reinvigorate Chinese communism and to provide Mao with more faithful successors with revolutionary experience.

Mao formed the Red Guards, a youth organization based in China's cities. Schools and colleges were shut down in order to allow China's youth to launch an attack on all traditional values, including the Confucian philosophy that had long shaped the country's heritage. By criticizing party officials, meanwhile, Mao believed that the young people would benefit both themselves and the officials by promoting rigorous communism. In fact, as the movement escalated, many Red Guards did not stop at verbally abusing officials but attacked or killed them.

The Cultural Revolution soon had negative results. As the Red Guards splintered into factions, anarchy and terror paralyzed the Chinese economy. Industrial production fell by 12 percent in only two years. To get scarce goods, many people turned to the corruption and bribery that communism was dedicated to eradicating.

Mao himself became alarmed by the Red Guards assault on Communist Party power, and in 1968 he decided to use the military to reinforce the party's dominance. Millions of Red Guards were moved from the cities to remote rural areas, lessening their influence. In the aftermath of the Cultural Revolution, when education again became more important than revolutionary fervor, the former Red Guards found themselves with little role in Chinese society. Meanwhile, China's bureaucrats became more tentative and less effectual as they sought to protect themselves from potential future punishments such as those of the Red Guards.

The question remained of Mao's successor. Defense minister Lin Biao was nominated but proved too eager to assume power. In 1971 he was killed during what the government claimed was an escape attempt after an abortive plot to assassinate Mao. To many supporters of the Cultural Revolution, the story of Lin's death was disillusioning. All their efforts and sacrifice, it seemed, had been elements not in an ideological conflict but in a simple power struggle. Mao looked to Chinese premier Chou En-lai and Deng Xiaoping, himself a victim of the Cultural Revolution, to lead China back toward some stability.

Young members of the Red Guard helping with the harvest outside Beijing read Mao's *Little Red Book* to a peasant during a work break.

cation that China's great famine had been mostly "man-made"—by Mao—stung the leader out of isolation to launch a new "socialist education movement." The main purpose of the movement was to guide China back onto the true road of communism. Its secondary aim was to get Mao back into power.

**The Cultural Revolution**

To help in his fight against the men who had replaced him, Mao turned to the army. Within a year of relinquishing power, he had begun to build up loyalty among the chiefs of the armed forces. In 1964, he turned his attention to ordinary soldiers.

Mao published his thoughts in the *Little Red Book*. Soldiers were instructed to read it and then spread its message throughout the country. The purpose of this activity was to convert millions of people—who knew little about Mao, Liu, or what went on in Beijing—into worshipers of Mao. So began the great convulsion called the Cultural Revolution, which erupted in 1966.

At the heart of the Cultural Revolution were the Red Guards. These soldiers and students were sent into every corner of China to preach the cult of Mao and root out supporters of Liu. Such a move represented a reversal in Chinese values. The country's traditional Confucian philosophy emphasized the wisdom of age, respect for one's elders, and the duty of the old to educate the young. One of Mao's aims in the Cultural Revolution was to undermine the influence of Confucianism in society.

To enable students to join in the revolution, schools and universities closed. The campaign devastated people's private lives. People who refused to bow before portraits of Mao or who were unable to quote from the *Little Red Book* lost their jobs. Liu's supporters were removed from their positions, tortured, and even executed.

By the middle of 1967, China was on the brink of civil war. Industrial production was severely disrupted, especially when Red Guards organized strikes by factory workers to demand higher wages. In response, Mao was forced to turn against the Red Guards that he himself had created. He established revolutionary committees in every province, staffed by army personnel and local party officials brought back from disgrace. Their appearance marked the end of the Cultural Revolution, although the movement was not officially declared to be closed until 1969.

For a few more years, tensions remained between those party members who thought that China should liberalize its economy and those who wanted the country to keep a hard-line communist stance. Mao's death in 1976 led to a complex power struggle, from which Deng Xiaoping (1904–1997) emerged as the country's new strongman in 1978. The following year, he achieved a major breakthrough in diplomatic relations with the United States.

A statue of a soldier standing on a bridge in Nanjing holds aloft a copy of the *Little Red Book* by Chairman Mao. All members of the armed forces were issued a copy of the work and encouraged to disseminate its contents to the largely illiterate peasant population.

## China and the United States

China's relations with the West began improving before Deng came to power. One reason for this development was a growing hostility between China and the Soviet Union, which dated to 1956. In that year, Stalin's successor, Nikita Khrushchev, had denounced his predecessor's tyranny. This censure upset Mao, who recalled Stalin's support when China had no other friends. Relations worsened in 1959, when Khrushchev refused to honor an earlier promise to supply China with nuclear weapons. In 1962, when a minor war broke out between China and India, the Soviet Union sided with India.

Faced with enemies everywhere, China worked to develop its own nuclear capacity and exploded its first atomic bomb in 1964. It thereby became the fifth country in the world—together with the United States, the Soviet Union, France, and Great Britain—to have nuclear weapons.

Possession of nuclear arms brought a new self-confidence. As tension with the Soviet Union grew, hostility with the United States eased. The process was helped by the Vietnam War (*see 8:1100*), which showed that the United States was not so invincible as it had seemed. Mao described America as a "paper tiger."

The Americans were happy to see relations sour between China and the Soviet Union, because it lessened the risk of a united communist threat to Western interests. The result was a dramatic shift in U.S. policy toward China. Since 1949, the United States had used its veto to block China's admission to the United Nations. In 1971, President Richard Nixon allowed China to become a member. The following year, Nixon became the first U.S. president to visit the communist mainland, signing agreements to lift many trade and travel restrictions between the two countries (*see 8:1102*). The thaw continued after Deng took control in 1978 and culminated when Washington and Beijing established full diplomatic relations the next year.

## Deng's Path of Reform

Deng set out on an ambitious path of domestic reform. Many policies of the old regime were overturned, including the long-standing emphasis on heavy industry. Deng planned to improve the lives of millions of ordinary Chinese by providing them more food, clothing, and household goods. He therefore set about creating conditions in which prosperity could occur.

Deng's government introduced incentives to get workers to produce more food and industrial products. Factory workers who increased their output earned bonuses. Peasants were allowed to sell crops on the open market for whatever price they could get. People were even allowed to own their own small businesses and to keep the profits they made for reinvestment. In the 1980s, for the first time, China began to manufacture large quantities of goods such as bicycles and sewing machines.

This new policy, called market socialism, heralded a more profound change: the gradual return of many areas of industry to private ownership. The results were encouraging. In the 1980s and 1990s, the Chinese economy grew faster—by 10 per-

Deng Xiaoping, pictured in 1963, was stripped of his prominent position in the Communist Party during the Cultural Revolution. He later regained his influence and, although he did not hold the technically most powerful posts in the government, was China's chief internal and foreign policymaker throughout the 1980s.

U.S. president Richard Nixon applauds a theatrical performance during his trip to China in February 1972, the first such visit by an American head of state.

cent every year in the 1980s—than almost any other economy in the world.

Some aspects of life hardly changed, however, particularly the communists' grip on power. Deng's attempts to modernize Chinese industry encouraged observers to believe that he would be open minded about political reform. Such reform, many people believed, was essential if prosperity was to improve the lives of most Chinese.

Carrying a helmet dropped by one of the soldiers who injured him, a worker makes his way through the crowd during the government repression of prodemocracy demonstrators in Tiananmen Square, Beijing, in March 1989.

High-rise apartment blocks dominate the city of Shanghai. In 1984, Shanghai was designated an open city in a successful effort by the Communist Party to encourage foreign investment.

In 1979, Deng gave his approval to the "democracy wall movement," when reformers used a wall in Beijing to put up posters calling for reform. Among their demands were greater democracy, the release of dissidents imprisoned during the Cultural Revolution, and the relaxation of state censorship. Deng declared that "the Democracy Wall is a good thing" because it encouraged people to drink from "the well of freedom." As a result, antigovernment handbills and pamphlets flooded China's towns and cities. Reformers gave speeches to huge outdoor meetings.

Deng soon recognized the danger in this explosion of public feeling and withdrew his support from the movement. In 1980, all nonparty newspapers were banned, as were democracy walls. The government returned to violent repression in a campaign against so-called spiritual pollution in the community.

### The Prodemocracy Movement

For a few months in 1989, the communists' grip on power seemed more vulnerable than ever before. Students and workers demonstrated in favor of democracy in Tiananmen Square, in the heart of Beijing. Behind their protest lay frustration that economic improvement had not raised the standard of living for most Chinese. Large numbers of people were also no longer willing to tolerate the oppressive nature of the communist government, which severely limited personal freedoms and regularly violated human rights. Faced with such criticism, the Chinese government sent in troops and tanks to crush the demonstration. Up to 2,000 protesters may have been killed in the process.

To many Chinese, the massacre of protesters in Tiananmen Square was nothing new. Many westerners were shocked because they knew little of Chinese history and because they had, like many Chinese radicals, put too much faith in Deng's apparent wish to modernize society. Other Chinese understood that modernization was one thing; a direct assault on communist rule, on the other hand, would never be tolerated.

In 1997, the British handed back to China the thriving colony of Hong Kong, which it leased in the nineteenth century. Hong Kong boasts a prosperous economy. Its citizens have become used to limited democracy and free-market capitalism. It remains to be seen whether Hong Kong can be reabsorbed and China itself modernized without profoundly disturbing the iron grip of the Communist Party (*see 9:1216*).

# Toward a United Europe

## *Forging Closer Ties*

In September 1946, Winston Churchill, Britain's wartime prime minister and one of the world's most respected statesmen, made a powerful speech on the future of Europe. Speaking in Zurich, Switzerland, he surveyed the plight of the continent in the aftermath of World War II. Churchill described a place where "a mass of tormented, hungry, care-worn and bewildered human beings gape at the ruins of their cities and homes."

This grim situation was the result of the chronic inability of European nations to live in peace with one another. Churchill's answer was "to re-create the European family and provide it with a structure under which it can dwell in peace, in safety and in freedom. We must build a kind of United States of Europe."

The vision of a united Europe that would overcome the divisions of the past inspired many people of Churchill's time, who had experienced the horrors of the world wars of 1914–1918 and 1939–1945. Many believed that the competition between nation-states, which had largely caused those wars, could not be allowed to continue. They also felt that many individual European states were too small and weak to hope to hold their own in the postwar world. Only by joining together in a larger unit could they compete with the might of the world's two great superpowers, the United States and the Soviet Union.

The attachment of Europeans to their distinctive national traditions, languages, and customs was also deep and powerful, however. Nationalism was a cause for

The blue flag of the European Union flies with the national flags of member countries outside the European Congress in Brussels.

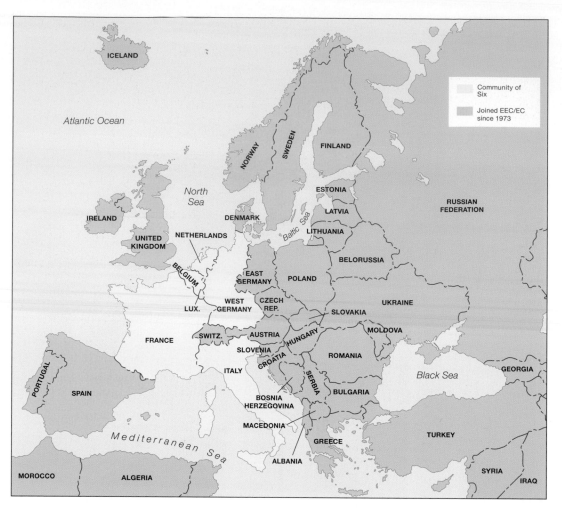

Six states began the move toward European integration but they were followed by others.

which millions had recently given their lives in war. The spirit of patriotism and sense of national, as opposed to European, identity was an immense barrier across the path to a United States of Europe. The same Churchill who spoke so eloquently of European union adamantly refused to submerge his own country in any such federation, saying of Britain, "We have our own dream and our own task, we are with Europe but not of it." The tension between national loyalties and the drive to European integration was to shape much of the politics of western Europe during the second half of the twentieth century.

### The Limits of European Unity

The limits of possible European unity were set initially by political divisions on the continent that had been brought about by the Cold War. By 1948, what Churchill dubbed an iron curtain separated the Soviet-dominated communist states of eastern Europe from the West. It was only in western Europe that progress toward integration could be made. Spain and Portugal were also excluded as possible members of a united Europe because in the postwar period they had right-wing, authoritarian governments. Such govern-

ments were incompatible with the liberal democratic principles embraced by the core states of western Europe.

As one of the victors of World War II, Britain was at first widely seen not only as a necessary partner in moves to build a new Europe but as the probable prime mover in the process. The British, however, proved more interested in maintaining their close political and economic links with the Commonwealth, largely made up of former British colonies, and in upholding the special relationship they felt they enjoyed with the United States. In the late 1940s, Britain was happy to promote bodies such as the Organization for European Economic Cooperation, the West European Union, and the Council of Europe, a series of virtually powerless forums for discussion between European governments, but it resisted any moves toward economic or political integration.

### Toward a Common Market

The prime mover behind the developments that eventually led to the European Common Market was the French economist and bureaucrat Jean Monnet (1888–1979). Monnet was an idealistic believer in a federal Europe, and he skillfully proposed

1190

A German steelworker empties a vat of molten metal at a plant near the Moselle River in this photograph taken in 1952. The Schuman Plan concentrated on coordinating steel and coal production in western Europe.

practical economic measures that appealed to European national governments. He also exploited these measures to the maximum in order to push toward a future goal of political integration.

Monnet first proposed the creation of a European Coal and Steel Community (ECSC), under an authority based in Luxembourg. The authority would coordinate these important industries in all mem-

European foreign ministers meet in Strasbourg, France, in 1949, in what was seen at the time as an assembly similar to a parliament of Europe.

European delegates pictured during the signing of the Treaty of Rome in 1957. The treaty brought into being the European Economic Community.

This European fighter aircraft is a successful example of the technological cooperation between states that accompanied political integration. EURATOM and the European Space Agency proved equally positive examples of the benefit of cooperation.

ber states, abolishing customs barriers between them, coordinating prices, and banning unfair competition. Monnet's proposal was taken up officially by the French government and announced in 1950 as the Schuman Plan, named for the French foreign minister and former prime minister Robert Schuman. The plan was received with enthusiasm by Belgium, the Netherlands, and Luxembourg, three countries that had already formed a customs union known as Benelux. The plan was also adopted by the West German government of Chancellor Konrad Adenauer (1876–

1967), and by Italy. Britain, however, remained aloof.

The ECSC was brought into existence by the Treaty of Paris in April 1951, and Monnet was appointed the first president of the high authority. The implications of the new organization were far more extensive than they first appeared, as it introduced the fundamental apparatus of European union. The ECSC was presided over by a council of ministers and an assembly of parliamentarians from the six member states. It also required the creation of a European court to oversee the legal terms of the agreement.

## The European Economic Community

At first it seemed that the six countries in the new community might make rapid progress toward more extensive unification. A treaty for a European defense community was signed in 1952, making arrangements to set up a unified European army, and plans for a European political community were drawn up. The treaty went too far for many national politicians, however. In 1954, the French parliament refused to ratify the defense treaty. The rush to integration ground to a halt.

Monnet once more took up the fight. He resigned as president of the high authority in order to set up a pressure group, the Action Committee for the United States of Europe. Support came from the Benelux countries, where ministers floated the idea of a European Economic Community (EEC) that would extend the coal and steel community to wider areas of the economy. This idea quickly found favor, and in March 1957 the Treaty of Rome created both the EEC and the European Atomic Energy Community (EURATOM), which provided for cooperation between member states in the development of atomic power.

## The Influence of de Gaulle

The shape of the EEC over the first decade of its existence was largely determined by a single Frenchman, Charles de Gaulle (1890–1970), who became president of

Two of the architects of modern Europe meet in Paris in 1963. At left is French president Charles de Gaulle, at right the German chancellor Konrad Adenauer.

In an outfit designed for the 1973 annual Ascot race meeting by her son, milliner David Shilling, Gertrude Shilling promotes British entry into the Common Market by displaying the names of the member states and the word in various languages for "cheers."

Gaullist rule in France coincided with a change of tack by the British. In 1961, under the government of Harold Macmillan, Britain belatedly decided to apply for membership of what the British habitually called the Common Market. Britain had begun to sense the dangers of exclusion from the major European markets for their exports and was acutely aware that its economic growth was lagging behind that of the six EEC countries.

Edward Heath, a British politician and noted pro-European, was given the task of negotiating the terms for British entry to the community. In 1963, however, de Gaulle unilaterally but decisively vetoed Britain's membership, a rejection he repeated in 1967. De Gaulle saw the British as being too closely linked to the United States. In his view, Britain would be a Trojan horse, surreptitiously introducing American influence into Europe.

De Gaulle also ensured that proposals for progress toward political union in Europe were again rejected in the early 1960s. He did approve, however, the setting up of the Common Agricultural Policy (CAP), which benefited French farmers through providing heavy subsidies for small producers. He also established a special relationship between France and West Germany that placed those two powers firmly at the hub of the new Europe.

## Expansion of the EEC

After de Gaulle fell from power in France in 1969, there were immediate moves to restart the drive for greater integration among the six EEC members and also to extend the EEC to include new members. With the pro-European Heath now prime minister in Britain, Britain duly repeated its application to join in 1971. Along with Denmark and Ireland, Britain entered the EEC on January 1, 1973. Norway also signed the Treaty of Accession, but the Norwegian people rejected membership in a referendum, and the country did not join.

Membership in the EEC also remained controversial in both Britain and Denmark, although Britain's membership was confirmed by a referendum that was held in 1975. There was no controversy in Ireland, which found both its prosperity and its national confidence boosted by joining the community.

Increasing the geographical extent of the EEC proved far easier than making progress toward economic or political union. In the 1970s, western Europe was badly hit by rising energy prices, fluctuating exchange rates, and competition from

France in 1958. De Gaulle was an ultra-nationalist who had no intention of submerging France in a federal Europe. De Gaulle was also, however, intensely anti-American, so he welcomed the EEC as a vehicle for countering the influence of the United States. The president was also concerned to cement close relations between France and Germany, which he saw as the key to preventing any repeat of the two world wars.

the fast-growing economies of the Asian Pacific Rim (*see 9:1209*). Struggling to cope with rising unemployment and inflation, national governments had little time for taking joint action with their community colleagues. The project for European union was put on the back burner.

## The Spread of Democracy

The 1970s brought significant advances for democracy in western Europe. Greece, Portugal, and Spain all shed right-wing authoritarian regimes and became liberal democracies. This development removed any political barrier to their joining the EEC, a move which their governments realized was desirable, because it offered the chance of rapid economic growth and would bolster their fragile democracies

There was a difficulty, however. The new candidates for admission were poorer than any that had so far belonged to the community, with large numbers of impoverished peasant farmers among their populations. Absorbing them into the EEC would alter its structure and balance of power. Nonetheless, Greece was admitted to the community in 1981, followed by Portugal and Spain in 1986. By then, the six original signatories of the Treaty of Rome had become twelve, covering all of noncommunist Europe except for Scandinavia, Switzerland, and Austria.

## On the Road to European Union

If anything, the widening of the EEC inevitably made the search for closer union even more difficult. More diverse countries

Two different faces of European agriculture: harvesting wheat by machine in France (*above*) and haymaking on a small farm in Portugal (*left*). As the Common Market admitted the poorer countries of southern Europe, discrepancies in agriculture and business made the community's economic and political balance increasingly difficult to maintain.

Oui VIVE L'EUROPE POUR QUE VIVE LA PAIX.

A 1992 French poster in favor of the Maastricht Treaty shows a cartoon Hitler crossed out and a slogan claiming that European union will guarantee European peace.

The high-speed Eurostar train links Paris and London through the Channel Tunnel. Inaugurated in 1994, this tunnel created the first roadway linking Britain and the European mainland.

defend their economic interests with a host of minor trade barriers and regulations. In 1986, they signed a Single European Act, committing themselves to creating a genuine European single market by 1992. People from member states would then, in effect, have the right to work, live, and do business anywhere in the community as if they were in their home country.

Delors followed this success with proposals for rapid progress toward economic monetary union, which would involve the creation of a European central bank and a single currency. Delors also proposed a social charter, which would provide workers throughout the community with the same labor union rights and right to a minimum wage, as well as other benefits.

These proposals for further integration were highly controversial. Among community leaders, British prime minister Margaret Thatcher became Delors's main opponent. In 1988, speaking at Bruges in Belgium, she delivered a ringing attack on the creation of a "European superstate exercising a new dominance from Brussels" and protested against the potential abolition of national identity in a European "conglomerate."

## Consequences of Political Change

The late 1980s and early 1990s were a time of rapid and sweeping changes in Europe. In 1989, communist governments collapsed throughout eastern Europe (*see 9:1243*). The following year, East and West Germany were unified in a single state with a population of over 80 million, more than 20 million higher than that of any other European country. In the same year, Thatcher fell from power, deposed as leader by her own Conservative Party, partly because of deep divisions within the party over moves toward European union. Then, in 1991, the Soviet Union disintegrated, a situation that challenged European leaders with a new world order.

To the surprise of many observers, the momentum of the drive toward European integration was sustained. German chancellor Helmut Kohl and French president François Mitterrand, the two key European leaders, agreed that the best way to cope with a united Germany, which threatened to unbalance Europe and reawaken old fears of German power, was to strengthen European unity.

In December 1991, meeting at Maastricht in the Netherlands, leaders of the twelve European Community states worked out an agreement on a European Union Treaty. This pact provided for staged

would now have to find their political and economic interests harmonized before integration became possible. During the 1980s, however, the political will to create a closer union clearly existed. It found expression in the appointment of former French finance minister Jacques Delors as president of the European Commission in 1985. Delors used his position to advance European integration more rapidly than at any time since the 1950s. Despite the principle of a common market, the member states of the community had continued to progress toward monetary union, which was to be achieved by 1999 at the latest. It also gave greater powers to the European Parliament, until then largely a token assembly, and introduced the notion of European citizenship, eventually to replace national citizenship.

Signed the following year, the Maastricht Treaty had been created by political leaders with little or no reference to the views of ordinary Europeans. There was disquiet in many member countries about the possible loss of valued aspects of national life. There was also concern about the loss of democratic control over decision making, which would increasingly move from national capitals and their parliaments to remote centers in Strasbourg and Brussels.

In Denmark, the majority of the population rejected the Maastricht Treaty in a referendum in June 1992, although it was narrowly approved in a new vote the following year. The treaty was almost rejected in France, where it was approved by the narrowest of majorities in a referendum in September. In Britain, no referendum was held, but popular disquiet was reflected in Parliament, where the treaty scraped through after a series of close-fought votes.

## The Question of Monetary Union

Apart from the lack of popular enthusiasm for the European Union (EC)—as the community was now renamed—the member states also had extreme difficulty meeting the criteria laid down for progress toward monetary union. The different national economies had to converge before a single currency could be made to work, bringing together their national expenditure, debt, and the value of their currency. Many experts predicted that convergence could not be achieved. It soon became clear that not all countries would be able to join the first wave of monetary union.

Meanwhile, the boundaries of the European Union continued to expand. In 1995, Austria, Finland, and Sweden joined, although the Norwegians again voted against membership and Switzerland also chose to stay outside. Other countries, however, were eager for admission. In 1998, negotiations on future membership were opened with Poland, Hungary, the Czech Republic, Estonia, Slovenia, and Cyprus. In addition, Turkey, Romania, Bulgaria, Latvia, and Lithuania expressed a wish to be admitted to the Economic Union.

On January 1, 1999, as intended, the euro became the official unit of currency in eleven of the fifteen European Union states. For the time being, Britain, Denmark, Greece, and Sweden stayed outside monetary union. More general debates continued within the EU about the pros and cons of membership, both in general and in detail. Fishing communities were angered by EU quotas that limited the amount of fish they

The offices of the European Parliament in Luxembourg.

A fisherman fills a holding tank on board a boat. Fishing quotas, in which the European Union limited the amounts of fish various countries could catch, were among the issues widely resented as examples of European interference in national traditions. Supporters of union argued that the quotas harmonized conditions for fishing operations throughout Europe.

could catch. Farmers were enraged by threats to cut subsidies they received under the Common Agricultural Policy. Nationalists feared the disappearance of symbols of nationhood, not least the national currency. Yet the European Union looked more likely to expand further than to fall apart.

## Toward a More United World

The development of the European Union was part of a worldwide trend in the latter part of the twentieth century to create a free market in goods, labor, and capital. In the 1990s, regional trade agreements and world trade accords flourished. The North American Free Trade Agreement (NAFTA) of 1993, for example, created a type of common market on the North American continent with Mexico, the United States, and Canada as member states.

The General Agreement on Tariffs and Trade (GATT) had provided a framework for the progressive liberalization of world trade since 1947. By 1994, when GATT was succeeded by the World Trade Organization (WTO), most of the attempts by nation-states to protect their economies with import barriers had, in principle at least, been banned.

The hostile reaction of some Europeans to European Union was mirrored by worldwide responses to the growth of regional and global free markets. These were unfavorable to the interests of many individuals and communities, who faced the threat of unfettered competition from cheap foreign goods and labor. National governments seemed increasingly powerless to defend their people against global market forces.

In Europe, it was a widely held belief that dismantling economic barriers would inevitably lead to greater political integration. Was the globalization of the world economy also a prelude to some form of world government? More than fifty years after its creation in 1945, it was obvious that the most likely candidate for the job, the United Nations, still fell far short of exercising world leadership. In addition, the disintegration of the Soviet Union and Yugoslavia in the early 1990s unleashed nationalist sentiments as powerful as had ever been seen. At the end of the twentieth century, the tension between the world's nation-states and nationalism on the one hand and an increasingly global economy on the other seemed inevitably to be a major theme for the new millennium.

# Latin America Since 1945

## The Fight for Self-Determination

In the decades following World War I, the United States took over from Great Britain as the chief international investor in Latin America (*see 7:973*). During World War II, the United States played a major role in fostering industrial development across Latin America, providing loans, expertise, and equipment to encourage industrialization. In exchange, every Latin American country with the exception of Argentina and Chile supported the Allied cause from early in World War II.

At the end of the war, Latin American countries, such as Brazil, Chile, Mexico, Colombia, and Uruguay, wholeheartedly set about switching their economic base from cash-crop agriculture to industry. The speed of the transformation created problems, however. Cities such as São Paulo, Brazil, received so many immigrants from the countryside that, in some areas, the exodus did not leave enough people to work the fields.

In order to finance new industries, Latin American states borrowed heavily from national and international banks. In order to attract customers, they often sold exports, such as sugar, cotton, cocoa, and coffee, cheaply. The economic basis of such industrial development remained fragile. It eventually brought crises as countries struggled to pay their debts. In the 1980s, for example, the annual inflation rate of Peru rose to 2,700 percent.

Photographed in Nicaragua in 1987, this group of antigovernment Contra rebels were on a recruiting drive in the northern province of Chontales. With U.S. backing, the Contras were well placed to benefit from popular dissatisfaction with the Sandinista government.

This map shows the countries of Latin America since World War II.

## Argentina

Argentina provides a revealing example of Latin America's difficulties since 1945. Between 1880 and 1930, Argentina became rich very quickly. So rapid was the economic boom that few people realized how fragile it was. Prosperity relied on a single export—beef—that was vulnerable to world demand. When that demand fell after the 1930s and Argentina rushed to industrialize in the same way as its neighbors, the resulting economic decline undermined the country's self-confidence.

To restore a sense of national pride, Argentines turned to a traditional Latin American ruler, the caudillo, or strongman. Historians see the army officer Juan Domingo Perón (1895–1974), who served two terms as president from 1946 to 1955, as the epitome of the military leaders who dominated much of Latin American politics between the 1950s and 1980s. Perón reorganized Argentina's society and economy to support the state. Generous social and economic reforms made the charis-matic president very popular with the workers. Perón also had the benefit of a wife, Maria Eva Perón (1919–52), or Evita, who inspired devotion among Argentines (*see 9:1202*). Evita worked to improve the position of women and the poor. Her early death from cancer, aged only thirty-three, robbed Perón of much of his popularity and helped precipitate his fall from power.

## American Domination Increases

The United States' involvement in Latin American politics continued after World War II. In 1948, the United States created the Organization of American States (OAS), ostensibly in order to continue the Good Neighbor policy first espoused in 1933 by President Franklin D. Roosevelt.

The United States had two principal ambitions in Latin America. It wanted to protect its investment in the region, particularly around the Panama Canal linking the Pacific and Atlantic Oceans. During the Cold War (*see 8:1083*), it also wanted to combat the spread of communism on the

1200

CUBA CORREOS 30

VISITA DE LEONID I. BREZHNEV ENERO 28 A FEBRERO 3 1974

The communist alignment the United States feared: this Cuban stamp from 1974 shows President Fidel Castro, on the right, with Soviet premier Leonid Brezhnev.

American continent. A populist revolution in Bolivia in 1952, in which armed miners and peasants helped overthrow the military government, suggested that U.S. concern was well founded. In Guatemala, meanwhile, the communist-supported Jacobo Arbenz was elected president in 1951. Arbenz launched a program of land reform, redistributing large estates among landless peasants. Some of the redistributed land supported banana plantations of the U.S.-owned United Fruit Company. In response to the measure and to growing communist influence in Arbenz's government, the U.S. Central Intelligence Agency (CIA) began to destabilize the Guatemalan government. In 1954, a CIA-recruited and -financed force of Guatemalan exiles invaded their

The National Congress Building stands in the city of Brasilia, which was created in the early 1960s by Brazilian architect Oscar Niemeyer as a purpose-built capital suitable for a thriving, forward-looking nation.

# The Story of Evita

Eva Perón (1919–1952), usually called Evita, became Argentina's most revered political leader, although she never held an official government post. Such was her hold on the Argentines that, even after her death, her supporters and enemies fought over her body for more than twenty years. Evita represented a new kind of political fame that bordered on religious fervor

María Eva Duarte had an undistinguished career as an actress before she began an affair with an ambitious military officer, Juan Perón, who by 1945 had become Argentina's vice president. When Perón was toppled from his position, his mistress and associates from Argentina's labor unions rallied workers in Buenos Aires to demand his release from custody. The pair were married before Perón successfully ran for president in 1946.

Evita won the adulation of Argentina's dispossessed, whom she addressed as *los*

Crowds throng the streets of Argentina to watch Eva Perón's funeral procession in 1952.

Eva Perón, photographed in about 1947. Since her death, Evita's story has been told many times, among them by the hit musical and movie *Evita* and the best-selling novel *Santa Evita*.

*descamisados*, Spanish for "the shirtless ones." When Perón won the election, his wife became unofficial minister for labor and health, awarding pay increases to the unions. She alienated the elite, however, replacing traditional social organizations with the Eva Perón Foundation, dedicated to establishing hospitals, schools, orphanages, and old people's homes. Evita was also responsible for giving women the right to vote in 1949 and making religious education compulsory in all schools.

By 1951, Evita was dying of cancer. She had made many enemies, especially in the army, who blocked her nomination as vice president. After she died the next year, her followers tried to have her made a saint by the Catholic Church for her efforts to improve the lives of the working class. Her opponents, concerned that she would become a rallying point for Peronists after the overthrow of her husband in 1955, stole her body and hid it in Italy for sixteen years before it was returned to her husband, then in exile in Madrid. Evita's body was repatriated by supporters but again removed by opponents before it was laid to rest in her family vault in a Buenos Aires cemetery.

homeland. The army refused to defend Arbenz, who resigned and was replaced by Colonel Castillo Armas. Armas's dictatorship, which canceled land reform and suppressed unions and peasant organizations, set a pattern for military dictatorships in Guatemala. Opposition to government rule in Guatemala became increasingly violent. In more than thirty years, some 100,000 people died in a civil war between the military regime and antigovernment guerrillas, the Guatemalan National Revolutionary Unity (URNG), that ended only in December 1996.

### The Cuban Revolution

Almost since its independence in 1899, Cuba had suffered political corruption. Although U.S. investment and tourism supported a thriving economy, wealth was distributed unfairly, and social injustice was common. In 1958, guerrillas overthrew the longtime dictator Fulgencio Batista. The leader of the revolution, Fidel Castro (b. 1926), who became president, was a Marxist communist who in 1961 abolished capitalism, nationalized foreign-owned businesses, and aligned Cuba with America's archenemy, the Soviet Union. Alarmed by the development, the United States tried to remove Castro from power. In 1961, the CIA backed an invasion by Cuban exiles that ended in failure at the Bay of Pigs. Numerous CIA plots to assassinate Castro included one using an exploding cigar.

For many Latin Americans, Castro became a symbol of resistance to the United States. He and his fellow revolutionary, the Argentine-born Ernesto "Che" Guevara (1928–1967), were adopted as figureheads for rebellion even by young people in the West. A traveler in Latin America in 1961 remarked that two faces were recognizable everywhere: the Virgin Mary and Fidel Castro.

In 1962, the potential siting of Soviet missiles in Cuba led to a crisis that nearly sparked a war (*see 8:1096*). The end of the crisis left the United States and its island neighbor as sworn enemies. The United

General Augusto Pinochet, photographed in 1986, was military dictator of Chile from 1973 to 1990. In the 1990s, legal challenges in various European countries attempted to bring Pinochet to trial for human rights violations during his time in office.

Women demonstrate against U.S. interference in Santo Domingo, capital of the Dominican Republic, in May 1965, when U.S. Marines suppressed a popular reformist rebellion in the country.

States imposed an economic embargo on the island. Cuba relied increasingly on Russian aid, and its economy was badly affected by the collapse of the Soviet Union in 1991.

### Alliance for Progress

Latin American politics remained subject to U.S. determination to prevent another Cuba. President John F. Kennedy's Alliance for Progress adopted a carrot-and-stick approach to Latin America, promoting social reform and economic development to prevent discontent that might lead to revolution. Any government whose reforms met with Washington's approval received U.S. funding; beneficiaries included Venezuela, Brazil, Argentina, Peru, Chile, and Colombia.

Colombia benefited the most from U.S. aid. Its political structure, based on a strict alternation of government between the two leading parties, protected economic growth by preventing any single group from gaining lasting control. Paralleling Colombia's growth were Brazil and Mexico. Such economies gained a huge advantage over those of Central American nations such as Guatemala, El Salvador, and Nicaragua, where development was inhibited by internal conflict between right-wing governments and left-wing guerrillas.

### The Overthrow of Salvador Allende

Latin America remained vulnerable to U.S. interference. In 1965, U.S. Marines suppressed a reformist rebellion in the Dominican Republic, which had for decades been ruled by dictators such as Rafael Trujillo. The United States feared that the rebellion had communist backing. Throughout the 1970s, Latin American dictators and military juntas, or councils, relied upon U.S. support. The United States, for its part, was eager to contain the guerrilla wars raging in Central America.

U.S. support did not preclude all change. In October 1968, General Velasco Alvarado seized power in Peru. Despite his call for radical land reform and the expropriation of a subsidiary of Standard Oil, a U.S. company, the Americans praised Velasco. Things were different in Chile, however, where in 1970, Salvador Allende (1908–1973) became the first elected Marxist president in the Western Hemisphere.

Allende wanted to reform Chile along the lines Velasco took in Peru. He embarked on a program to improve housing, health services, and education for the poor. The speed of change polarized Chile's left and right wings, however, and tension grew. In 1973, the CIA backed a right-wing military uprising against Allende, led by General Augusto Pinochet (b. 1915). Allende died in the fight to defend the presidential palace in Santiago, and Pinochet established a dictatorship that lasted until 1990. Chile's economic progress under his rule was soured by the murder of thousands of political opponents by right-wing death squads.

### The Rise of Military Dictatorships

By the mid-1970s, Latin America was largely ruled by military juntas or dictators. Only Colombia, Venezuela, and Costa Rica had democratically elected governments. The reasons behind the proliferation of undemocratic military rule were complex. Some historians argue that the appearance of military regimes, even in advanced countries such as Brazil and Chile, was a result of the breakdown of state organization under the pressures of continuing industrial development.

Military intervention in politics was not new in Latin America, although the emphasis on economic development was. Organized, often violent, opposition to military rule was also increasingly effective. In Brazil and Argentina, disregard for the democratic process led to internal wars in the early 1970s between the army and pro-democracy guerrillas, who were often students. Many people "disappeared" in Chile and Argentina as the military rulers systematically killed any opposition. It was not until the late 1990s that Argentine generals even admitted to the crimes they committed during the so-called dirty war.

## The Wars in Central America

The presidency of Ronald Reagan from 1981 to 1989 marked a new phase of U.S. involvement in Central America, particularly in Nicaragua. The Somoza family had ruled Nicaragua since 1937, propped up by U.S. support. In 1979, President Jimmy Carter withdrew that support in response to repeated violations of human rights. The Sandinista National Liberation Front (FSLN), formed in 1962, toppled the Somoza dynasty and formed a government. Carter offered financial help to the new regime, but incoming president Reagan froze all aid. Reagan's administration believed that the left-wing Sandinistas posed a communist threat not just to Central America but to the whole continent. The U.S. government approved financial aid for the Contras, the right-wing guerrilla movement that emerged to oppose the Sandinista government, and even trained and armed Contra fighters.

## The Iran-Contra Affair

The full extent of U.S. involvement in Nicaragua came to light only in 1986. Unknown to Congress, Reagan's National Security Council (NSC) had sold arms to Iran, a country that the United States officially boycotted as a sponsor of international terrorism. Some of the $48 million

that Iran paid for the arms was passed to the Contras by Lieutenant Colonel Oliver North, a member of the NSC, to allow the guerrillas themselves to buy arms. The scandal became known as Irangate or Contragate. Reagan, who denied knowl-

U.S. Blackhawk helicopters prepare to land troops during the 1983 invasion of Grenada.

A picture of Fidel Castro and a work by the North Korean leader Kim Il Sung feature among the evidence of communist influence in Grenada the United States used to justify its invasion.

1205

edge of the scandal, left office before a full investigation could be concluded. In Nicaragua, the Sandinistas were voted out of power in 1990 by a disillusioned public tired of waiting for promised changes.

## Guatemala and El Salvador

In Guatemala and El Salvador, successive military governments waged war not only on opposition guerrillas but also on their respective indigenous populations. The Guatemalan government accused the highland Indian tribes, who make up over half of Guatemala's total population, of aiding the guerrillas. Government forces hunting guerrillas were reported to have exterminated entire Indian villages.

Guatemala's neighbor, El Salvador, experienced twenty years of civil war as right-wing government forces fought the

Little more than a child, this antigovernment guerrilla was photographed in El Salvador in 1983.

guerrilla opposition. Few opponents dared speak out against the government's death squads or the army's use of torture on civilians. One man who did so, Oscar Romero, archbishop of San Salvador, was murdered in his cathedral as he celebrated mass.

By the mid-1980s, the wars in Central America had reached deadlock. In 1986 and 1987, the Costa Rican president, Oscar Arias, developed a peace plan. The heart of the Arias plan was the principle that Central American governments should solve their own problems through negotiation, without external interference.

All the same, U.S. involvement in Latin America continued throughout the 1980s. In 1983, American troops invaded Grenada, a British dependency. In December 1989, U.S. troops landed in Panama, where the army's commander in chief, General Manuel Noriega, had unconstitutionally seized power. Noriega was forcibly removed and sent for trial in the United States on drug-trafficking charges.

## The 1990s

In the last decade of the twentieth century, as military governments failed, many parts of Latin America enjoyed the best opportunities since independence to achieve democracy. As early as 1983, for example, Argentina had returned to civilian government, partly thanks to the humiliation of the military junta by defeat in a conflict with Great Britain over the Falkland Islands. How far Latin America had changed was seen in Venezuela in 1992, when an attempted military coup failed to oust the elected government.

Guerrilla groups and antigovernment forces, such as the FMLN in El Salvador, demobilized. The Sendero Luminoso, or Shining Path, guerrilla movement, active in Peru since the 1980s, ceased operations by 1995 following the arrest of its leader, Abimael Guzmán, in September 1992. The exception to the general scaling down of guerrilla movements was Mexico.

The Institutional Revolutionary Party (PRI) had ruled Mexico since 1946. By the 1990s, opposition to the PRI had grown amid charges of corruption and ballot rigging. On January 1, 1994, a guerrilla group—named the Zapatistas after Emilio Zapata, a hero of the 1910 Mexican Revolution (*see 6:744*)—took control of several towns in the state of Chiapas. The Zapatistas demanded social justice for indigenous Mexicans, setting out their demands on a dedicated internet site.

Mexico's problems were compounded in the mid-1990s by an economic crisis that

led to recession and inflation. Latin America's economies in general remained fragile. The reasons for the fragility included political instability, overreliance on a limited range of exports, and the crippling repayment of the loans that funded the rapid industrialization in the middle of the century. In the 1970s and 1980s, the region suffered hyperinflation that was only defeated in the 1990s by austerity measures. The Mexican crisis, however, was followed by a global economic collapse that spread to Latin America in 1999. Brazil, the region's largest economy and the world's eighth largest, devalued its currency in an attempt to avoid recession.

The mothers of the "disappeared," the victims of Argentina's dirty war, demonstrated every week in Buenos Aires in an effort to discover the fate of their vanished loved ones.

Mourners fill a church in San Salvador at the mass funeral of six Jesuit priests murdered by gunmen in 1989 for speaking out against the government. 1207

Against a sea of Nicaraguan flags, Violeta Chamorro arrives in Managua's National Stadium to take over from the Sandinista president Daniel Ortega in April 1990. Chamorro was Latin America's first female head of state.

## Religious and Social Concerns

The latter half of the twentieth century saw the Catholic Church redefine its role in Latin America. In many countries, the church no longer aligned itself with conservative interests. Instead it championed the poor, calling for land reform and criticizing dictators in El Salvador and elsewhere. This manifestation of Catholicism, known as liberation theology, emerged in the 1970s as priests went to work in villages, where they led peasant agitation for social reform. In the 1970s and 1980s, military governments increasingly murdered priests and nuns who condemned human rights violations. Meanwhile, an evangelical branch of Protestantism, brought to Latin America from the United States, increased its membership dramatically. Evangelical churches became common in countries such as Mexico and Brazil.

## The Role of Women

The political upheaval of the late twentieth century led to changes in the position of women in traditionally patriarchal Latin American societies. Women proved as capable as men of being guerrilla soldiers and fighting for change; they were also just as likely to "disappear" as the victims of right-wing death squads. With the murder of so many men in Central America, some women became the sole supporters of their families and of each other. In Buenos Aires, Argentina, meanwhile, mothers of the disappeared marched every Thursday outside the parliament long after the end of the "dirty war," demanding to know what had happened to their children. The radical change in women's position was reflected in works by many women writers. In 1990, Violeta Chamorro, the widow of a murdered newspaper publisher, defeated the Sandinistas in Nicaragua to become the first female president in Latin America.

## A New Problem

By the late 1990s, many countries of Latin America had made the transition from agricultural to industrial economies, including Argentina, Chile, Brazil, Mexico, and Uruguay. Such countries had increasingly little in common with their more agricultural neighbors, such as Bolivia, where the population remained predominantly rural and poor. Subsistence farmers, who owned little land because of a lack of wholesale land reform, found it difficult to make a living from growing coffee and other crops.

Farmers' search for a more profitable crop had international repercussions. The leaves of the coca shrub are used to produce cocaine. Throughout Bolivia, Peru, Ecuador, and Colombia, farmers grew coca leaves to sell to cocaine manufacturers, often in Colombia. International attempts to restrict the trade were not effective. Coca is part of Andean culture, and neither growing nor using its leaves is illegal in these countries. Indians traditionally use the shrub to alleviate altitude sickness. Bolivian miners, for example, chew coca leaves or drink coca tea to help them cope with their demanding working conditions.

For the rest of the world, particularly the United States, simply banning the coca industry is impracticable. Measures to make growing coca economically unattractive for farmers have largely failed. In the 1980s, for example, Colombian drug barons' profits from illegal cocaine manufacturing and trafficking exceeded the total legitimate income of the nation. The drug barons themselves were a serious challenge to the authority of the legitimate government. Elsewhere in Latin America, however, constitutional democracies supported fragile industrialized economies.

# The Economies of the Pacific Rim

*From Boom to Bust*

In the first half of the twentieth century, as in preceding centuries, the world economy was focused largely around the North Atlantic. Most of the world's largest centers of trade and industry were located in the eastern half of the United States and in western Europe. The second half of the century, however, brought a shift of focus to the Pacific Ocean. The world's fastest-growing industrial and trading regions have been on the western seaboard of the United States and along Asia's Pacific Rim.

### The Japanese Economic Miracle
The most remarkable success story belongs to Japan. Defeat in World War II left the country physically devastated and occu-pied by U.S. forces under General Douglas MacArthur. The U.S. administration endowed Japan with a democratic constitu-tion. It also introduced economic reforms, mainly in agriculture, where small farmers were given ownership of land they had worked as tenants of absentee landlords.

In 1950, conflict with communist China in the Korean War convinced the Americans that a strong Japan could act as a bulwark against the spread of communism. When U.S. occupation ended in 1952—American bases remained in Japan to provide a defense against any communist attack—it was still not expected that Japan would become a major industrial power. In 1954, U.S. secretary of state John Foster Dulles

An electronics store in Taipei, capital of Taiwan, embodies the technological development that underlay the booming Pacific Rim economies in the postwar period. From an initial emphasis on producing cheap goods, the Asian economies tended to focus more on quality and innovation, particularly in modern sectors, such as electronics.

A symptom of Japan's ruined economy, this social worker, photographed in 1946, dealt with hundreds of destitute Japanese every day.

(1888–1959) assured Congress that Japan was not capable of manufacturing export goods of sufficient quality to compete in the United States.

Dulles was not entirely correct. Although the Japanese initially focused on producing cheap rather than high-quality goods, 1954 was the year when Japan's economic output recovered to its prewar level. Over the next three decades, the Japanese achieved economic growth rates that astonished the world. Between 1954 and the late 1960s, the Japanese economy grew at over 10 percent a year, faster than that of any other major country. By 1968, Japan led the world in the production of a whole range of goods, from motorbikes to transistor radios, cameras, and even pianos. Companies such as Sony, Yamaha, and Honda became internationally respected. Japanese

Motorcycle fans around the world wanted machines made by Japanese companies such as Kawasaki and Honda, which produced this 1997 Firestorm.

shipyards built almost half the world's merchant vessels. Japan's economic growth continued through the world economic recession of the 1970s, despite the fact that the country was dependent on imported petroleum, a commodity whose price increased astronomically during the decade. By 1987, Japan had the second largest industrial economy in the world after the United States and a higher per capita gross national product (GNP) than America. The respective GNPs, which measure the total value of goods or services produced by each citizen a year, were $17,000 per capita compared with $16,000.

## The Causes of the Miracle

The Japanese economic miracle depended on numerous factors. One was the close partnership between government and business. Although Japan was a democracy, the Liberal Democratic Party (LDP) was consistently in power throughout the period of economic growth, creating a high degree of political stability. The LDP governments encouraged people to save, providing the capital for industrial investment at low interest rates. They also actively promoted export-oriented industries by providing tax breaks and maintaining an exchange rate for the yen that made Japanese goods competitive in foreign markets. For their part, Japan's large business corporations invested heavily in research and innovation in emerging industries, such as electronics. They also developed advanced production and management techniques to get the best out of their workforce.

A number of other factors also helped Japan's growth. U.S. bombing during World War II had destroyed much industrial machinery, so the country rebuilt from scratch using the latest technology. Japan also maintained only small armed forces in the postwar period, because it could count on U.S. protection. By keeping military spending low—only 1.6 percent of the national income in 1958, for example—the Japanese government could concentrate investment in economic development.

Government spending on welfare was also low at a time when many Western economies were developing expensive welfare states (*see 8:1078*). This was partly because Japanese families traditionally performed tasks, such as care of the elderly, which elsewhere were now entrusted to the state. It was also because Japanese corporations, such as Toyota, offered lifelong employment and many of the benefits provided by a welfare state. In return, such corporations commanded great loyalty from their workers.

## Rising Standards, Rising Competition

Having initially used cheap labor to produce cheap goods, by the 1960s, the Japanese had managed a transition to higher wages and the production of high-quality goods. Living standards improved dramatically. From 1960 to 1967 alone, average wages doubled. By the end of the 1960s, the average Japanese owned more and better consumer goods than the average western European and was not far behind the average American. Almost all the products sold in Japan were manufactured by the Japanese, so the expanding domestic market provided a solid base for export-led economic growth.

By 1987, Japan exported $100 billion worth of goods a year more than it imported. Japanese businesses had become massive investors of capital in foreign countries, including the United States and Asia. One result of Japanese investment in Asian countries was to stimulate competi-

Japanese companies earned a reputation for technological innovation. Radios, like this palm-sized model made by Sony in the early 1980s, grew smaller. Similar technology later brought innovations such as palm-top television sets and handheld VCRs.

A telling sign of economic superiority, a poster for the Japanese Sony corporation looms over pedestrians in the Chinese capital, Beijing.

tion for its products. By the 1980s, countries such as South Korea and Taiwan had become a serious challenge to Japan in world markets.

## Korea: From War to Boom

Korea was a Japanese colony from 1910 to 1945. After Japan's defeat in World War II, Korea was divided into a Soviet zone in the north and a U.S.-occupied zone in the south. The two zones evolved into the communist state of North Korea and pro-Western South Korea. In 1950, North Korean forces invaded South Korea but were driven back by an American-led United Nations army. When UN forces threatened to take over North Korea, China intervened to drive them back. In 1953, the war ended with an armistice that virtually restored the border between North and South to its prewar position.

The war, following on from the depredations of Japanese colonial rule, left both halves of Korea impoverished and eco-nomically backward. South Korea had to spend large sums of money, which could have been invested in economic development, on armed forces to defend against any new invasion from the north. At the end of the 1950s, South Korea ranked among the world's poorest countries. It was industrially undeveloped, with four out of five of its people working in agriculture.

## Economic Renewal

In 1960, mass demonstrations forced the resignation of South Korea's authoritarian ruler Syngman Rhee, who had run the country since 1948. A year later, General Park Chung Hee took power and launched an ambitious drive for rapid industrialization, based on government planning and financial rewards for exporters. He also normalized relations with Japan, which had been upset by Korean demands for financial compensation for Japanese colonial rule. Improved relations brought an influx of Japanese investment to South Korea.

The South Korean economy grew by a remarkable 9 percent a year from 1962 to 1992. By the late 1980s, the country had one of the ten largest industrial economies in the noncommunist world. Seoul and other cities swelled as peasant farmers migrated to become urban workers. Average living standards in South Korea in the 1980s were not as high as in Japan but were similar to those of poorer west European countries such as Portugal. This growth produced a remarkable transformation in people's lives. In 1970, only one in twenty South Koreans owned a television set, for example, but by 1985, TV ownership was almost universal. Lower wages enabled Korean corporations such as Samsung to imitate Japanese products but manufacture them at a lower cost, creating a competitive advantage in export markets.

South Korea's success was not without cost. To finance its growth, the country borrowed heavily, building up a massive international debt. The bill for imports of food and machinery was huge. Politics remained unstable. Park Chung Hee was assassinated in 1979. His successors were also military men. Chun Doo-Hwan gov-

Stylish and relatively cheap models, like this No. 1, allowed Korean car maker Daewoo to find a lucrative market in the Western economies.

Political unrest continued to threaten Korea's economic development. Protesters with smoke bombs broke up this rally in support of Roh Tae Woo in Seoul in 1987.

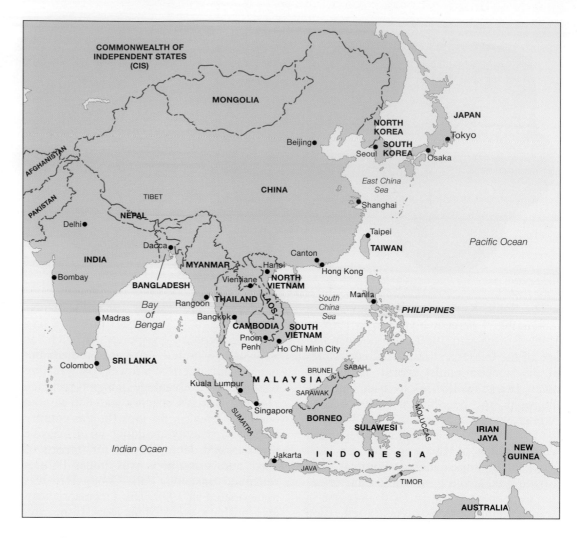

This map shows the Pacific Rim and the main countries benefiting from high rates of economic growth.

erned from 1980 to 1988, and Roh Tae Woo from 1988 to 1993. Both were later convicted of serious offenses after democratic civilian government was established in South Korea in 1993.

## Chinese Tigers

By the 1990s, Japan and South Korea together accounted for about 15 percent of the world's total income and 10 percent of world trade, although they had only 3 percent of the world's population. Similar economic success came in the island state of Taiwan and in Hong Kong, a British colony until 1997 (*see 9:1216*).

Like Korea, the island of Taiwan, then known as Formosa, was a Japanese colony until 1945. When communists took power in mainland China in 1949, the defeated Kuomintang leader Chiang Kai-shek chose Taiwan as the new base for his Chinese Republican government (*see 7:944*), which continued to claim to represent all of China. About two million Kuomintang supporters took refuge in Taiwan, imposing their rule on its existing population.

Taiwan's economy was in crisis. In 1949, inflation was 3,000 percent a year. The population worked mainly on the land,

with rice and sugar as the chief exports. Because mainland China remained a constant threat of invasion, there was little incentive for the Taiwanese to invest in long-term business development.

By 1961, however, the government had brought inflation under control at 3 percent a year. It then embarked on a drive to promote export-oriented industries, providing cheap credit for industrialists and setting up special "export processing zones," where businesses could operate free of bureaucratic red tape and taxes. As a result, between 1960 and 1972, the economy grew at around 10 percent a year, a rate almost equal to that in Japan. By 1979, Taiwan's national product per head was six times that in communist China. Workers enjoyed better food, housing, and health care than their equivalents in mainland China.

An even more striking example of entrepreneurial ability was provided by the British colony of Hong Kong. Like Taiwan, Hong Kong absorbed several million refugees from Chinese communist rule in 1949. Whereas in Japan, Taiwan, and South Korea, the state played a leading role in promoting economic growth, in Hong Kong growth relied on business acumen

Container ships in Kaohsiung, Taiwan, in 1991. The port is the third-largest container port in the world, mainly thanks to the island's export trade with the United States.

and hard work alone. Hong Kong businesses built up a thriving industrial and trading economy but, above all, made the colony one of the world's leading financial centers. The glittering skyscrapers of Hong Kong Island bear witness to an extraordi-

nary success story, based on exploiting the need of the global economy for so-called offshore banking, free from the controls imposed by national governments.

The spectacle of Chinese economic success in Taiwan and Hong Kong had a pro-

Old and new mix in Taipei in this juxtaposition of a traditional gateway built in memory of Chiang Kai-shek and a modern office building that reflects Taiwan's economic prosperity.

# The Special Case of Hong Kong

On July 1, 1997, Britain handed Hong Kong back to the Chinese. The British had won control of the island of Hong Kong at the end of the Opium War of 1842. In 1898, they negotiated with China a ninety-nine-year lease on other islands and a mainland region, the New Territories. With the expiry of the lease, the entire colony passed back to Chinese rule.

Circumstances had changed the relationship between Britain and China. The establishment of British influence came during a period when many Western powers were eager to gain trading entrepôts in China. Now the colonial powers had largely departed. China itself had undergone a revolution that left a communist government in power, ideologically opposed not just to the capitalist spirit that underlay Hong Kong's business but also to the freedom of expression associated with liberal democracies. Many Hong Kong Chinese had fled there after the communists took power in China in 1949, bringing technology and capital to promote economic development.

The colony provided a model on China's doorstep of the unrestrained free market that communism condemned. Hong Kong's wealth depends on its position as a trade center, benefiting from its natural harbor and lack of import taxes, and as a financial center. It is also home to thriving manufacturing industry, particularly in textiles and electronics, and is a center of the movie industry.

Hong Kong's postwar economic success depended on unregulated exploitation of labor, which provoked social unrest. Conditions improved with legislation in the late 1960s. In 1973, a stock market crash slowed Hong Kong's economic advance, which returned as relations improved with China.

Those improving relations reassured some Hong Kong citizens of the colony's future within China. Others protested that China's 1989 crackdown on pro-democracy demonstrations augured badly. China, for its part, proposed a notion of "one country, two systems," in which Hong Kong and other economic development zones could encourage capitalist economics while the rest of China remained insulated from the accompanying ideas of liberal democracy.

Victoria Harbor, lying between Hong Kong Island and the mainland. The anchorage provided the early stimulus for Hong Kong's development as a port.

found influence on the Chinese communist government. From the end of the 1970s, after the failure of various attempts at a planned economy, China began to seek a pragmatic approach to economic development. The special economic zones set up along the coast of mainland China in the 1980s were modeled on Taiwan's export processing zones. The fastest-growing special economic zone, Shenzhen, was just across the border from Hong Kong and soon developed at least a superficial resemblance to the island colony, with its dense concentration of high-rise office buildings. By the 1990s, Hong Kong and Taiwanese businesses had become major investors in mainland China.

## Southeast Asia

The countries of Southeast Asia generally had more natural resources than Taiwan, South Korea, or Japan but were slower to experience the postwar economic transformation sweeping the eastern Pacific Rim, largely as a result of political struggles that held back development. The countries of Indochina, for example, Vietnam, Laos, and Cambodia, were devastated by warfare and revolution. In Indonesia, however, the battle for decolonization and the socialist policies put in place by President Sukarno, who ruled from 1945 to 1967, also brought economic chaos, poverty, and mounting foreign debt. The Chinese minority that ran much of Indonesia's business was systematically discriminated against. In 1965, it was the victim of large-scale massacres. In Malaysia, communist insurgency held back development in the 1950s, as in the early 1960s did armed confrontation with Sukarno's Indonesia.

The stimulus for economic growth in Southeast Asia eventually came from outside. The first impetus was money from Japan, which during the 1950s paid reparations to the Southeast Asian countries it had occupied during World War II. These payments were followed by the purchase of raw materials, such as Indonesian oil and Malayan rubber, needed for Japan's expanding industries, which also found a growing market for their exports in the region. In the 1970s, Japan began direct investment in Southeast Asia to set up factories exploiting the relatively low cost of local labor.

## A Growing Confidence

The second great stimulus to Southeast Asian economies came with the massive involvement of the United States in the war in Vietnam (1965–1973). Thailand and the Philippines, for example, became crucial

Workers assemble Sony televisions in a plant in Vietnam's Ho Chi Minh City, formerly known as Saigon. Japanese investment has funded economic development in many countries throughout the region.

U.S. bases for the war effort, as well as sites for "rest and recreation" for American service personnel. Bangkok, the Thai capital, was transformed in only a few years from a quiet backwater into an overcrowded modern city seething with vice. This was only one of the most visible examples of changes spreading throughout the region as a result of the American presence.

In 1967, at the height of the Vietnam War, Thailand, Malaysia, the Philippines, Singapore, and Indonesia—which was now under the rule of the pro-Western President Suharto—created the Association of South-East Asian Nations (ASEAN). The association's purpose was to promote economic and political cooperation within its membership, and its formation was a sign of growing political stability and economic confidence. By that date, for example,

These workers, photographed in Jakarta, Indonesia, in the 1980s, are putting together tennis shoes for Reebok. The decision of corporations such as Reebok to take advantage of cheap labor in Asia led to factory closures in the United States and concern for future employment prospects

Singapore had already begun an economic boom. Under the authoritarian but dynamic rule of Lee Kuan Yew's People's Action Party, Singapore seceded from the Malaysian Federation in 1965. The independent state was soon well on its way to becoming a second Hong Kong, a small but intensely active hub of industry, finance, and trade.

The other countries of Southeast Asia found it more difficult to achieve rapid growth or true political stability. Only in the 1990s did Thailand, Malaysia, and Indonesia begin to be spoken of as new "Asian tigers." By then, such countries were engaged in their own versions of the economic miracle. Their ambitions were symbolized by the construction of Petronas Towers in the Malaysian capital, Kuala Lumpur. On completion in 1997, the towers replaced Chicago's Sears Tower as the world's tallest building.

### The Growing Influence of Asia

As Asia developed economically in the postwar period, its growing influence spread to Australasia and the west coast of the Americas. In 1945, and for some years afterward, Australia and New Zealand still considered themselves outposts of the British Commonwealth. Culturally and economically, their closest links remained with their former colonial ruler, Great Britain. In 1966, however, Australia abolished a race-based immigration policy that had encouraged European settlers but excluded Asians. Within a short time, by far the largest proportion of new immigrants came from Asia. At the same time, Australia and New Zealand reoriented their economies toward trade with the Pacific

Not everyone benefits equally from the economic miracles of the Pacific Rim. Because wages remain low, many people still live in crowded slums like this one in Jakarta, capital of Indonesia.

zone rather than Europe. By the 1980s, Japan had become the largest trading partner of both Australia and New Zealand and was also a major source of investment in their domestic economies.

The western seaboard of the United States and Canada showed a similar tendency toward growing trade and cultural links with the countries they faced across the Pacific. By the 1990s, for example, California's top trading partners were Japan and the Asian tigers. Japanese corporations owned many of the state's banks and numerous industries. The economic reorientation was underlined by the effects of increased immigration from Asia. By 1991, for example, a quarter of the population of Vancouver, in Canada's British Columbia, was of Asian origin, largely Hong Kong Chinese. Large Chinese, Japanese, and Korean communities automatically looked to trade with their compatriots across the Pacific.

## Globalization

The economic rise of the Asian Pacific Rim reflected and contributed to the phenomenon of globalization. This term describes the process by which cultural and particularly economic factors operate on a global

rather than a national or even continental scale. Modern technology and communications mean that someone in Little Rock, Arkansas, and someone in Bangkok, Thailand, might not only buy the same brand of TV set but watch the same shows while drinking the same soda. Multinational corporations, meanwhile, could build plants anywhere, allowing them more effectively to seek out the cheapest resources and labor.

Asia's economic emergence had a profound impact on the rest of the world. On one level, the availability of cheap goods made available to the developing world many of the same material possessions, such as cars or stereo systems, as those common in the developed world. On another level, the tiger economies exploited their poorer neighbors in the search for cheaper labor, as in Sony's establishment of plants in Vietnam.

Asia's economic success brought job losses in the West. In some cases, however, it also created employment, such as when Asian corporations opened factories in the West to satisfy export markets in the United States and Europe. Western corporations learned from the imaginative research and development programs and

Swimming pools dominate an aerial photograph of an exclusive suburb in the Australian city of Brisbane. Taking advantage of its geographical proximity to Asia rather than its cultural links with western Europe allowed Australia to benefit from the prosperity of the Pacific Rim.

1219

aggressive marketing strategies that characterized Asian businesses. Japanese management techniques and industrial relations were highly influential throughout the world, with their stress on efficiency, job satisfaction, and mutual obligations between company and worker.

## The Political Question

Asia's economic miracle was based to a large extent on adopting the free market and the consumer-oriented values common in the West. There was, however, no corresponding adoption of the values of liberal democracy that many people in the West associate with a flourishing free-market economy. The governments of the Pacific Rim display rather a continuity with the region's own traditions of social organization. Japan's democracy in fact usually returned the same party to government. China remains a totalitarian communist state whose poor record on human rights is tolerated by countries such as the United States largely because of its potential value as a trade partner. South Korea, Indonesia, Thailand, Vietnam, and Malaysia are virtual one-party states. Political opposition is routinely oppressed or legally silenced. A state such as Singapore uses a strict penal system and harsh laws to proscribe the daily lives of its citizens. Such conditions, governments argue, are a price worth paying for prosperity, but that argument only works as long as the prosperity exists.

The Tokyo Stock Exchange, photographed here in 1987, was rocked in the following decade by the collapse of some of Japan's largest businesses.

## Problems and Fears

As the end of the millennium approached, prosperity in Asia threatened to disappear. The Asian Pacific Rim entered a troubled period following four decades of optimism and unrestrained growth. In 1997, the rapid growth achieved by Thailand, Malaysia, and Indonesia was called into serious question by deep financial depression. The apparent success of all three had been built on huge debts that they could not repay, and much of the money had been invested unwisely and unproductively. The value of their currencies collapsed, as did many banks and other businesses.

What was dubbed Asian flu proved catching. The collapse of currencies in Southeast Asia quickly had a similar effect in South Korea, which was revealed to have equally serious problems of heavy debts and faltering economic performance. As large Korean banks and industrial corporations went bankrupt, the International Monetary Fund (IMF) had to step in with an emergency loan to prevent the complete collapse of the economy. Because of the close links globalization had forged between the world's economies, the Asian downturn had profound effects elsewhere, disrupting business and trade from the United States and Europe to Brazil.

The sudden loss of prosperity also had a profound political influence. In Indonesia, for example, economic crisis led to large-scale political unrest as protests against the crash broadened into protests against the political system. In 1998, Sukharno's successor, President Suharto, resigned after thirty years in power.

## Outlook for the Future

The end of the economic miracle dragged Japan into a recession made worse by the crash elsewhere in Asia. When the Japanese firm of Yamaichi, one of the ten largest financial businesses in the world, went bankrupt in November 1997, there were predictions of an even more dire depression in Japan. In April 1998, the president of Sony declared, "The Japanese economy is on the verge of collapsing."

Predicted catastrophes do not always occur. Hong Kong is a case in point. In July 1997, by agreement between Britain and the government in Beijing, the colony was reabsorbed into communist China. Prophets of doom, who predicted a mass emigration of the business community, were confounded. The city not only continued to function much as it had done before; compared with some of its neighbors, it weathered the economic crisis relatively well. At the end of the twentieth century, it remained to be seen whether the other countries of the Pacific Rim could get their own economic miracles back on course.

# Postcolonial Africa

## *The Struggle for Autonomy*

In the decade from 1956 to 1966, a wave of decolonization brought independence to thirty-three African countries that had been European colonies since the so-called scramble for Africa of the late nineteenth century (*see 6:817*). Apart from a few small territories, the north and center of the continent came under African rule, although white rule continued in southern Africa.

The new African-ruled states gained independence within the arbitrary borders created by European mapmakers and politicians who had sometimes simply drawn lines on blank maps of the continent to divide their empires. Such borders did not always reflect the ethnic, religious, or historical distribution of peoples. In the early 1960s, some African independence leaders, such as Ghana's Kwame Nkrumah (1909–1972), argued that the old colonial borders should be abandoned in favor of

progress toward a United States of Africa. This view found little support. Independent African countries set up the Organization for African Unity (OAU) in 1963, but despite its name the OAU pledged itself to uphold existing national borders.

As European administrations withdrew from Africa, the new African states all suffered, in varying degrees, from a shortage of administrative skills. The drive to independence in most countries had been led by an educated elite that constituted only a small proportion of the population. This elite had to staff government bureaucracies and armies, replacing colonial officers and administrators as quickly as possible. A recent university graduate might find himself or herself appointed as ambassador to Washington; a high-school principal might suddenly be put in charge of a large government department.

Kenyan prime minister Jomo Kenyatta and Britain's Prince Philip wave to cheering crowds in Nairobi during Kenya's independence celebrations in December 1963. Kenyatta had previously been imprisoned by the British for eight years for terrorism.

A distant tree is the only sign of life in a Mauritanian landscape during a drought in 1973. The effects of Africa's natural disasters were often exacerbated by political incompetence and corruption, which themselves often reflected the external influences of the Cold War or of neocolonialism.

## The Cold War and Neocolonialism

Africa's inexperienced new rulers faced immense problems. Above all, they found that political independence did not always bring true independence. External factors still shaped African life. Independence coincided with the height of the Cold War (*see 8:1099*), when the United States and the West vied with the Soviet Union and its allies for global dominance. New African governments looked to one of the sides in the Cold War for economic support. The major powers, for their part, were eager to extend their influence and afraid to allow their opponents to gain an advantage. Western governments supported the racist regime that emerged in white-ruled South Africa, for example (*see 9:1228*), partly in order not to allow an opportunity for the Soviet Union to gain influence there.

African countries were also affected by what is known as *neocolonialism*. The word describes a situation in which previous colonial powers retain continuing importance in independent countries. Former French colonies in western Africa, for example, such as Senegal and Mali, remained linked to France by membership in the French Community, which dealt with shared affairs. Other former colonies, particularly those with rich resources such as minerals, remained dominated by Western business interests. European companies often retained control of mines and communications concerns, for example.

Most Africans believed that colonial exploitation had kept Africa poor and that decolonization would be followed by a sharp rise in national wealth and living standards. On the whole, however, the continuing influence of neocolonialism prevented this rise. As external governments and businesses competed for influence, occasionally through force or corruption, they weakened the new African states, whose priorities were rarely based purely on the welfare of their citizens.

Economic performance in Africa differed widely from one country to the next, but in general, living standards at best remained stable and often declined. There were several reasons. One was rapid population growth. There were some 277 million Africans in 1960. By 1990, the figure had risen to more than 648 million. With so many additional mouths to feed each year, it was difficult to bring about a rise in the standard of living.

## Economic and Other Problems

Before independence, the vast majority of Africans earned their living from farming, and the continent was largely self-sufficient in food. A combination of population growth and migration from rural areas to the cities transformed this situation. In the first three decades of independence, the size of most capital cities increased tenfold. Both Lagos, the capital of Nigeria, and Kinshasa, the capital of Zaire—now the Democratic Republic of Congo—had populations of more than three million by the 1980s. Independent Africa became overwhelmingly dependent on food imports.

There were other social problems. Many communities remained isolated and undeveloped, with little access to clean water or medical provision to combat even common diseases. Education was available only to elites, and literacy levels remained low. Communications and transport infrastructures remained barely adequate. In some areas, local warfare left large regions abandoned because of land mines.

Shoppers throng a street market in the Nigerian capital, Lagos. In many countries, independence coincided with a growth in urbanization as people flocked to Africa's capital cities.

In the late 1970s, the countries of Africa were the first to suffer a new scourge, Acquired Immune Deficiency Syndrome, or AIDS. The disease, which removes the body's ability to fight off infections, was expected to kill millions of Africans.

## Financial Crises
The new African governments were generally not interested in encouraging farm output. Urged on by outside political and economic pressures, they tended to hold to the belief, fashionable in the 1960s and

Copper ingots gleam in the sun at a mine in the Katanga region of Zaire. Many mines remained in the hands of Western concerns that encouraged Katanga's unsuccessful bid for independence in 1960.

Many of the countries of Africa became independent in the decades after World War II. The map shows the dates of independence.

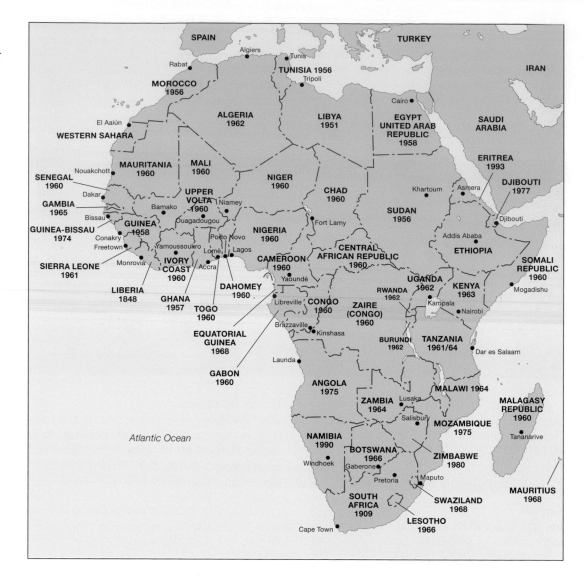

1970s, that state planning and the development of heavy industry were the road to economic development. They borrowed heavily to invest in massive power and industrial projects, building up debts that, by the 1980s, they could not pay. Meanwhile, they remained at the mercy of world markets over which they had no control. The rapid rise in world oil prices in the 1970s, for example, bankrupted African states that had to import all their petroleum.

As had proved the case in other regions, such as Latin America (*see 7:973*), countries overdependent on the export of a single commodity were especially vulnerable to falling prices on the world market. Zambia, which earned most of its foreign income from copper exports, was almost ruined by a fall in copper prices.

African economies were also damaged by extreme weather conditions. Countries in a band across northern Africa from Mauritania and Mali in the west to Ethiopia and Somalia in the east suffered years of disastrous drought. The effects of low rainfall were made worse by the impact of pop-

ulation growth, which led to the overexploitation of fertile grazing land, in places turning it into desert. However, the famines that ravaged parts of Africa—for example, Ethiopia in the 1970s and 1980s and southern Sudan in the 1990s—were all to varying degrees the result of political upheaval rather than weather alone.

Many of Africa's worst economic problems were, at their roots, traceable to the difficulty of establishing and maintaining orderly government. After independence, most African leaders sought to overcome that difficulty by rapidly abandoning democracy. They established single-party states and suppressed political opposition. One justification for this was fear of ethnic divisions, or "tribalism." The populations of the new countries were often ethnically diverse, comprising peoples who spoke different languages and had different customs and beliefs. The single party was generally presented as representing the "national" interest against the divisive influence of tribalism. In most cases, however, the government represented the dominance of one

Women in the Ghanaian capital, Accra, celebrate the downfall of President Kwame Nkrumah, in 1966. A hero of independence, Nkrumah later alienated supporters with his dictatorial ambitions.

ethnic group over the others. For example, the Kenyan population included Kikuyu, Masai, Luo, Baluhya, and Kamba people, as well as several smaller tribal groups. Kenya's leader at independence, Jomo Kenyatta (c. 1894–1978), was a Kikuyu, and the Kikuyu became dominant in his party, which ran the Kenyan state.

## Postindependence Disillusion

In many countries, the ruling party became the pathway to privilege, and inefficiency and corruption thrived. Some of the men hailed as heroes at independence were soon being reviled by their own people, as in the case of Kwame Nkrumah. Leading Ghana to independence in 1957, Nkrumah was acclaimed as a spokesperson for Africa on the world stage. However, in 1960, he declared himself president for life and banned all opposition parties. When Nkrumah was overthrown in a military coup in 1966, Ghanaians celebrated in the streets.

Ghana was far from alone in moving to military rule. In the two-year period of 1965 and 1966 alone, army officers also seized power in Nigeria, Algeria, Zaire, the Central African Republic, Upper Volta, and Burundi. Other countries that experienced substantial periods of military government included Uganda, Sudan, and Ethiopia. In some ways, the swing toward military government was an acknowledgment of the fact that the army was sometimes the most efficient and the least partisan force in a country.

## Idi Amin and Uganda

Some of Africa's original independence leaders proved durable rulers and figures of political and moral stature. This was true, for example, of Julius Nyerere (b. 1921) in Tanzania, Kenneth Kaunda (b. 1924) in Zambia, and Léopold Senghor (b. 1906) in Senegal. However, the image of independent Africa in the eyes of the world was characterized by the actions of a few megalomaniac dictators, such as Jean Bokassa (1921–1996) of the Central African Republic. The most notorious dictator was Idi Amin (b. 1924/1925), president of Uganda.

Amin was a largely uneducated Muslim who rose through the ranks of the army to become commander of the Ugandan armed forces after independence. He seized power in 1971 and ruled as dictator for eight years. Amin instituted a reign of terror, killing thousands of political opponents, including individuals such as the Anglican archbishop of Uganda. He ordered massacres and expelled the country's 80,000 Asians under duress, confiscating their businesses and property. Under his brutal regime, the Ugandan economy collapsed. Amin was removed from power by a Tanzanian invasion force in 1979.

## African Conflicts

Some parts of postcolonial Africa were the scene of destructive civil wars. One began in 1960, when the vast territory of the Belgian Congo was rushed to independence under the young radical Patrice Lumumba (1925–1961), with inadequate

Refugees in a camp in Sudan gather to collect food supplies. Since 1956, the Sudan has been devastated by the effects of civil war and famine caused by recurrent droughts. 1225

Grim-faced residents of the Belgian Congo arrive in Brussels in July 1960 after fleeing the violence that followed the colony's rapid transition to independence.

Nigeria, the most populous country in Africa south of the Sahara, also experienced an attempted secession. The country was divided by ethnicity and religion, with Muslim Hausa and Fulani in the north, Anglican and Muslim Yorubas in the west, and Catholic Ibos in the east, as well as a host of smaller ethnic groups. In 1966, a military coup sparked the massacre of thousands of Ibos in the Muslim north. The Ibos fled to their homeland in the east.

In 1967, the Ibo military governor, Colonel Chukumeka Ojukwu, declared the eastern region independent as Biafra. The Nigerian government of General Yakubu Gowon fought to subdue the rebellion. Food supplies in Biafra soon began to run out, and mass starvation set in. At least a million people are thought to have died before Biafra surrendered in January 1970.

The longest-running regional revolt in Africa occurred in Sudan, where southern Christian and animist peoples, non-Christians who attribute conscious life to natural phenomena, are ruled by Muslim northerners who control the capital, Khartoum. Guerrilla warfare began in southern Sudan at the time of independence in 1956 and, despite intermittent periods of relative peace, was still going on in the late 1990s.

## Switching Sides in the Cold War

Ethiopia had only experienced colonial rule briefly, after its conquest by Mussolini's Italy, between 1936 and 1941. In 1973, a devastating famine provoked widespread protests against the Ethiopian ruler, Emperor Haile Selassie (1891–1975). Selassie's government, supported by the United States, was held largely responsible for the people's suffering. In 1974, Selassie was overthrown in a coup and replaced by a left-wing military junta.

By 1977, the military regime faced armed independence movements in the northern province of Eritrea and in the region of Ogaden, supported by the neighboring country of Somalia. Keen to extend its influence, the Soviet Union, which already supplied aid to Somalia, flew in military supplies and Cuban troops to Ethiopia. In response, the Somalis broke with Moscow. On the global scale of the Cold War, Ethiopia and Somalia had effectively switched sides. The fighting in Eritrea continued, and famine ravaged the country throughout the 1980s. In 1991, the military junta was overthrown; Eritrea finally became independent in 1993.

The Cold War confrontation was more acute in southern Africa, where the struggle

preparation. Four days after independence, the Congolese army rebelled against its Belgian officers, and Belgian troops were sent in to evacuate Belgian civilians. At the same time, the mineral-rich areas of Katanga and South Kasai declared themselves independent of the Congo. The breakaway states were financed by Belgian mining interests and defended by mercenaries.

The Soviet Union threatened to send troops to help Lumumba, who called on the United Nations to preserve the Congo. A UN force reunited the country, but the Katangan revolt continued until 1967, and Lumumba himself was murdered by his enemies. Revolts rumbled on in the Congo until an army strong man, General Joseph Mobutu, took power in 1965. In search of African authenticity, Mobutu renamed the Congo Zaire and himself Mobutu Sese Seko. He led one of Africa's most corrupt regimes until he was overthrown in 1997.

for liberation from white rule was still raging in numerous countries during the 1970s. In 1974, a left-wing revolution in Portugal led to the rapid granting of independence to the Portuguese colonies in Africa, which had already been the scene of prolonged guerrilla warfare by liberation movements. Angola and Mozambique became independent under Marxist governments in 1975, although both countries continued to be involved in civil wars.

In Angola, the Marxist People's Movement for the Liberation of Angola (MPLA) was pitted against two other nationalist forces, the National Union for

the Total Independence of Angola (UNITA) and the National Front for the Liberation of Angola (FNLA). White-ruled South Africa, with the support of the United States, had invaded Angola in support of the FNLA, which had lost out in the independence deal. With Soviet logistical support, Cuban troops were rushed into Angola to repel the South African invasion. As a result of their support, the Marxist government survived. South African raids into Angola continued throughout the early 1980s, however, in an effort to overcome Namibian resistance forces that were operating from Angola.

Fearful of the expansion of communist influence, the United States encouraged South Africa to maintain a subversive campaign in Angola and Mozambique. With support from both the Americans and South Africans, UNITA guerrillas of Jonas

Robert Mugabe, photographed at a conference in Rome in 1978, was the leader of the guerrilla Patriotic Front movement in Rhodesia. In 1980, a peace settlement with the government led to the creation of Zimbabwe under a coalition government led by Mugabe. In 1987, Mugabe turned Zimbabwe into a one-party socialist state.

Terrorist or freedom fighter, depending on one's point of view: this guerrilla fought for the Patriotic Front of Robert Mugabe, which eventually won independence for Rhodesia as Zimbabwe in 1980.

# South Africa and Apartheid

South African police stand over a protester shot during the 1960 Sharpeville riots against the hated pass laws. Seventy people died when the police broke up the demonstration.

In South Africa, the white minority attempted to hold on to power in the face of a growing black population and internal and international protest by erecting a society segregated on racial grounds.

New president Nelson Mandela grasps hands with his predecessor and vice president F. W. de Klerk during the inauguration ceremony for the first multiracial government on May 10, 1994.

Racial segregation had existed in South Africa long before 1948, when the ruling National Party declared a policy of *apartheid*, an Afrikaans word for "apartness." Two years later, the Population Registration Act classified South Africans as Bantu, or blacks; Colored, or of mixed race; and white. Asian, a fourth category, was added later. The same year, the Group Areas Act set up business and residential areas for each race. Nonwhite citizens were forced by bitterly resented "pass laws" to carry documents to authorize their presence in white areas.

Other laws, meanwhile, forbade social interaction between races, created separate public facilities and schools, and barred nonwhites from certain jobs and from participation in government. Later, South Africa created ten homelands for black Africans and granted them a certain amount of self-government, but they remained dependent on South Africa.

Although the South African government had the power to suppress internal dissent, criticism was constant. Protest was led by the African National Congress, or ANC, and by black labor unions, with the support of some whites. Protests against the regime became increasingly violent as terrrorists began bombing campaigns against whites. Violence also broke out between the ANC and the Zulu Inkatha movement. ANC leaders were jailed, while the police assumed greater powers and turned illegal death squads against what they saw as their enemy.

South Africa found itself internationally isolated. Many people overseas boycotted South African goods, and in 1985, both Britain and the United States imposed economic sanctions. In 1986, South Africa abolished the pass laws, but significant change came only with the presidency of F.W. de Klerk in 1990 and 1991. Accepting that apartheid could not continue, de Klerk dismantled the apparatus of apartheid and enfranchised all racial groups. An election in 1994 returned an ANC majority government led by Nelson Mandela, himself imprisoned from 1962 to 1990. Apartheid was formally over, but the effects of decades of repression left many black South Africans condemned to misery, poverty, and squalor, even as the rising black middle classes began to share in their nation's prosperity.

Savimbi, based among the Ovimbundu of southern Angola, maintained an insurrection until the 1990s, devastating Angola's economy. A similar South African–backed guerrilla force brought Mozambique virtually to its knees in the 1980s.

## The End of White Rule

Despite the devastation wrought upon Angola and Mozambique, their independence did signal the beginning of the end for white rule in southern Africa. In Rhodesia, the government of white settlers, headed by Ian Smith (b. 1919), had unilaterally declared independence from the United Kingdom in 1965. Until 1975, the Rhodesian regime coped easily with African nationalist guerrillas fighting for black majority rule. Once the Patriotic Front guerrilla movement was able to operate from bases in independent Mozambique, however, the tide turned in the nationalists' favor. In September 1979, Smith was forced to accept a British-brokered agreement for fully democratic elections. Rhodesia became independent as Zimbabwe in 1980, under Patriotic Front leader Robert Mugabe (b. 1924).

## South Africa

South Africa, where Dutch immigrants first settled in 1652, remained a seemingly permanent stronghold of white rule in Africa. During the postcolonial period, from the 1960s into the 1980s, successive South African governments not only failed to liberalize the racial segregation, called apartheid, that guaranteed white domination, but made it progressively harsher.

An attempt by South Africa's main anti-apartheid movement, the African National Congress (ANC), to mount a campaign of peaceful protest against the apartheid regime was crushed. In one incident, police shot and killed seventy unarmed demonstrators at Sharpeville in March 1960. When the ANC subsequently adopted a policy of armed resistance, its leaders were driven into exile or arrested, which was the fate of Nelson Mandela (b. 1918), who was sentenced to life imprisonment in 1964.

Under pressure from international public opinion that condemned its racial policies, South Africa became an outcast, banned from international organizations and barred from sporting and cultural events. However, it continued to enjoy the quiet support of many Western governments, who saw it as a bulwark against the spread of communism, and of multinational companies, which found it a profitable place to do business.

The first cracks in the apartheid state began to appear in 1976, when young blacks took to the streets in the township of Soweto to fight the heavily armed security forces with sticks and stones. When riots flared again in the 1980s, it was evident that the apartheid regime could only be kept in place by constant police oppression. White rule was also threatened by the changing balance of the country's population. At the start of the twentieth century, one in four South Africans had been white; by the end of the century, whites would make up only one in ten of the population.

In 1990, South African president F. W. de Klerk decided that apartheid would have to end. He released Nelson Mandela from prison, lifted the ban on the ANC, and began to dismantle the racial segregation laws at the heart of apartheid. Despite threats of a white backlash and conflict between the ANC and the Zulu Inkatha movement, South Africa staged democratic multiracial elections in April 1994. After a landslide victory for the ANC, Mandela became South Africa's first black president.

U.S. troops man a communications post during the UN operation in Somalia in 1992. Operation Restore Hope, which aimed to remove control of food supplies from local warlords, ended in withdrawal when it seemed that UN forces would be dragged into a long, unwinnable conflict.

In a photograph that captures hope for the future, South African children pose in an integrated elementary school classroom in 1996. During the apartheid era, children of different races had to attend separate schools.

## Hope and Despair

The end of apartheid in South Africa was the most hopeful development in Africa during the 1990s. There were also signs of economic progress. In the 1980s, the inability of the African states to pay their debts put most of them effectively under the control of the World Bank. To save costs, states were forced to slim down their state apparatus, liberalize their economies, and encourage small farmers. These moves had a generally favorable effect on economic activity, although the cuts in state spending reduced further the already low standards of health care and educational provision in most of the continent.

In politics, meanwhile, pressure to introduce multiparty democracy and civil liberties increased in the 1990s. However, some African states continued to be ravaged by armed conflicts. In Algeria in 1992, for example, a military government blocked elections that would likely have been won by an Islamic fundamentalist movement, the Islamic Salvation Party. The fundamentalists declared war on the government, initiating a terrorist campaign that was met with counterterror by the authorities. Massacres, violence, and persecution became a daily reality for the Algerian population.

Some African countries descended into chaos, such as Sierra Leone and Liberia in West Africa and Somalia in East Africa. The overthrow of Somali president Muhammad Siyad Barre in 1991 allowed warlords to exercise such authority as existed, disrupting the distribution of food to such a degree that famine threatened millions. Under the banner of the United Nations, U.S. and other troops intervened in 1992 and 1993 to guarantee food supplies. They withdrew shortly after as the Somali quagmire threatened to suck them down.

## War in Rwanda

In 1994, a horrific ethnic struggle broke out in the small central African state of Rwanda. Rwanda and neighboring Burundi both had a minority of Tutsi inhabitants and a majority of Hutu. In 1972, several hundred thousand Hutu in Burundi had been massacred by forces of the Tutsi government. In Rwanda, meanwhile, the Hutu discriminated against the Tutsi minority.

By 1994, Rwanda was in the grip of a civil war as rebels of the Tutsi Rwandan Patriotic Front fought the Hutu-dominated government. In April of that year, Rwandan president Juvenal Habyarimana and his Burundian counterpart were both killed when their aircraft was shot down.

The unexplained event triggered a systematic campaign by Rwandan government militias to exterminate both the Tutsi minority and Hutu opponents of the regime. About half a million people were killed, as UN soldiers in Rwanda and the international community failed to intervene. The massacres were followed by military victory for the Tutsi rebels. In fear of retribution, four million Hutu fled the country to refugee camps in Zaire, although most returned home in 1996.

At the end of the twentieth century, Africa remained the world's most war-torn continent, the poorest continent, and the continent most adversely affected by AIDS. Many parts of Africa also remained dependent on western countries and institutions, such as the World Bank, that restricted African states' ability to address their own problems.

# Islamic Ferment

*The Rise of Militant Fundamentalism*

In 1979, revolution swept Iran, one of the most powerful countries in the Muslim world. Driven by religious fundamentalism, or the strict adherence to the basic principles and practices of Islam, the revolutionaries overthrew a state they believed embodied corrupt Western values. The revolution deposed the shah, or emperor, and replaced him with a radical government committed to the application of Islamic law and a way of life based on religious principles. The new Iran was hostile toward some countries of the non-Muslim world, particularly the United States, which it saw as a threat to its beliefs.

At the time, it seemed possible that the Iranian revolution might be the start of a wider uprising of the Muslim peoples of the Middle East and a war against Western interests and influence. By the end of the millennium, however, the impact of militant Islamic fundamentalism had proved to be less dramatic than once seemed likely, though radical religion remained a force to be reckoned with in the Muslim world.

## Historic Origins

An important reason for the rise of Islamic fundamentalism lay in the humiliation suffered by the Muslim world in the nineteenth and early twentieth centuries. Once-powerful Muslim countries were treated with contempt by the major Western powers, who defeated their armies

Their hair covered to observe Islamic laws on modesty, a troop of female Iranian mujahideen, or guerrilla fighters, parades at a military base in 1991.

1231

Young Egyptian girls attend school in this photograph from the mid–1960s. For some strict Muslims the growing adoption of Western fashion and hairstyles represented only the first step toward an inevitable decline in Islamic practices.

In January 1979, at the start of the revolution in Iran, demonstrators pull down a statue of Reza Shah Pahlavi, father of the then ruler of Iran.

in war and dominated their governments. Some Muslim states, including Egypt, Iran, and Turkey, responded by modernizing; they adopted Western laws, customs, and technology. This process inevitably led to secularization, or the reduction of religious influence on political and social life.

For many Muslims, however, modernization and secularization were simply further forms of humiliation at the hands of the West. Several movements called on Muslims to revolt by rejecting the influence of the West and returning to the true values of Islam. A prominent example was the Muslim Brotherhood, a powerful influence in Egyptian politics in the 1940s.

Anti-Western resentment in the Muslim world grew after the creation of the state of Israel in Palestine in 1948 (*see 8:1131*). The formation of Israel appeared as another act of Western imperialism in the Middle East. To complicate matters, the strong support given to Israel by the West, especially the United States, undermined the Muslim governments that maintained links with the West. Those governments were increasingly condemned at home as traitors to both Palestine and Islam.

## Revolution in Iran

From the 1950s to the 1970s, Iran was one of the foremost of the modernizing Muslim countries. Its ruler, Shah Mohammad Reza

Pahlavi (1919–1980), was an enthusiastic follower of the West. He used Iran's oil revenues to fund industrialization, freed women from the constraints imposed by traditional Muslim society, and created a modern education system. For these very reasons, the Shah found himself opposed by some of Iran's religious leaders. He made himself increasingly unpopular by crushing dissent in a remorseless way.

The majority of Iranians are Shiites, followers of the Shia rather than the Sunni branch of Islam. Shiite mullahs, or religious leaders, traditionally enjoyed great political influence and privilege in Iran, especially around the northwestern city of Qom. The shah's reforms met with the mullahs' disapproval, especially when he redistributed much land belonging to religious institutions to peasant farmers. In 1963, the authorities suppressed anti-government demonstrations at Qom; the next year, a prominent Shiite mullah, Ayatollah Ruhollah Khomeini (1900–1989), fled into exile in Europe.

Despite religious unrest, the shah's regime seemed secure. The United States saw him as an ally against communism in the Cold War and supplied him with large amounts of military hardware. Rising revenues from oil paid for a Western consumer lifestyle for Iran's urban elite and for grandiose state projects. Under the surface, however, discontent was growing, pro-

Jubilant Iranians salute Ayatollah Khomeini, in the center of the picture with the white beard, on his return from exile on February 1, 1979.

1233

voked both by a widening gap between rich and poor and by resistance to the social changes brought about by the shah's modernization. Iranians feared the shah's notorious secret police, the Savak, who used torture and intimidation to discourage critics of the regime. Many Iranians also resented the shah's close friendship with the United States, principal supporter of the hated Israel. University students, themselves the product of the shah's educational reforms, became militant in their criticism of the government. Ayatollah Khomeini kept up a stream of propaganda from exile, urging revolt against the shah in fiery speeches that were recorded and secretly circulated inside Iran on cassette.

## An Islamic State

In early 1978, religious students in Qom were killed by police during an antigovernment protest. Demonstrations against the deaths set in motion a spiral of protest that, by the end of the year, saw a million or more demonstrators flooding almost every

day onto the streets of the capital, Tehran. Striking workers closed down the oilfields, and soldiers eventually refused to fire on the crowds. In January 1979, the shah fled the country.

On February 1, the seventy-eight-year-old Khomeini returned from exile to scenes of wild jubilation and became the leader of an Islamic republic. The new regime soon banned alcohol, pop music, mixed-sex bathing, and all other signs of "Western decadence." Women were forced to adopt Islamic dress, and a strict code of Islamic justice was approved.

The new theocracy proved as ruthless toward opponents as the previous regime, but its aims had overwhelming public support. The mullahs preserved this support by maintaining a propaganda campaign that whipped Iran into religious fervor.

The United States paid for supporting the shah by being denounced as the "Great Satan." It tried to remain on good terms with the Iranian government, but in November 1979, after the exiled shah entered the United States for medical treatment, Iranian militants stormed its embassy in Tehran, taking fifty-two staff members hostage. In spite of appeals from world leaders, the Iranian government refused to intervene. The hostages were released in January 1981, after 444 days in captivity.

## Islam Divided

The West was deeply concerned that the Islamic revolution would spread, but Iran was ill-placed to lead a general anti-Western movement in the Middle East. In the first place, Iran is ethnically and linguistically different from most of its neighbors. Iranians, who speak Farsi, are of Persian descent, while most of their neighbors are Arabs, speaking Arabic. The Arab states of the Persian Gulf themselves had long feared the power of Iran. Like the West, they, too, regarded the Islamic revolution with considerable fear.

Another reason why Iran could not muster wider support in the Muslim world was its Shiite faith. The majority of Muslims elsewhere were Sunnis. A history of schism and conflict between the two branches of Islam made it highly unlikely that any Sunni Muslim would heed the Shia mullahs of Iran. The brief 1979 occupation by armed Shiite extremists of the Great Mosque in Mecca, one of Islam's most holy places, caused great resentment among Sunni Muslims.

If anything, the Iranian revolution brought conflict to the Muslim world rather than unity. In 1980, it sparked the eight-

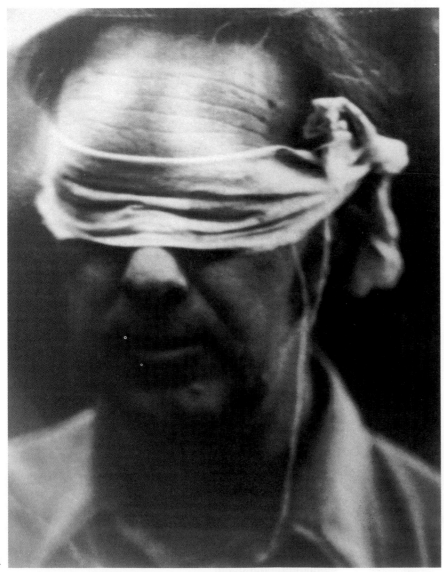

One of the U.S. embassy staff taken hostage by militant Muslims is paraded before the cameras in November 1979. A U.S. rescue attempt in April 1980 failed when equipment malfunctioned and two aircraft collided, killing eight soldiers and making the United States seem weak and ineffectual in the face of terrorism.

year Iran-Iraq War. Saddam Hussein (b. 1937), who became president of Iraq in 1979, resented calls by Khomeini for Iraqi Shiites to revolt. Saddam also saw in Iran's revolutionary turmoil a chance to expand Iraqi territory. In September 1980, Iraqi forces invaded Iran, advancing on the oil center of Abadan. The Iranians refused to surrender and fought back determinedly.

By the end of 1982, the Iranians had forced the Iraqis back across the border. Neither side could achieve a decisive advantage, however. In tactics that echoed those of World War I, massed infantry of each side advanced across open ground in the face of machine guns and artillery. Casualties mounted to hundreds of thousands on both sides. The Iranians eventually gained the upper hand through sheer force of numbers, but it was clear that they were incapable of finally defeating Iraq, especially when Saddam used chemical weapons, against which Iranian troops had little or no defence. In 1988, the combatants agreed to a ceasefire, allowing both to disengage with their honor relatively intact.

## Inspiration for Revolutionaries

Despite deep divisions within the Muslim world, the Iranian revolution did inspire Islamic fundamentalists in several other countries. Various groups emerged in Egypt, for example, as violent successors

to the Muslim Brotherhood. In the nineteenth century, Egypt had been the first Middle Eastern country to modernize itself along Western lines. From 1956 to 1970, President Gamal Abdel Nasser had followed a successful policy that married a pro-Western stance with Egypt's Muslim

Boys study with their teacher in a Muslim school in India in 1984. Islam places great stress on education, seeing literacy as an important means of reinforcing faith.

This monument stands in the Iraqi capital, Baghdad, in honor of the hundreds of thousands of Iraqis who lost their lives in the ultimately unsuccessful war against Iran.

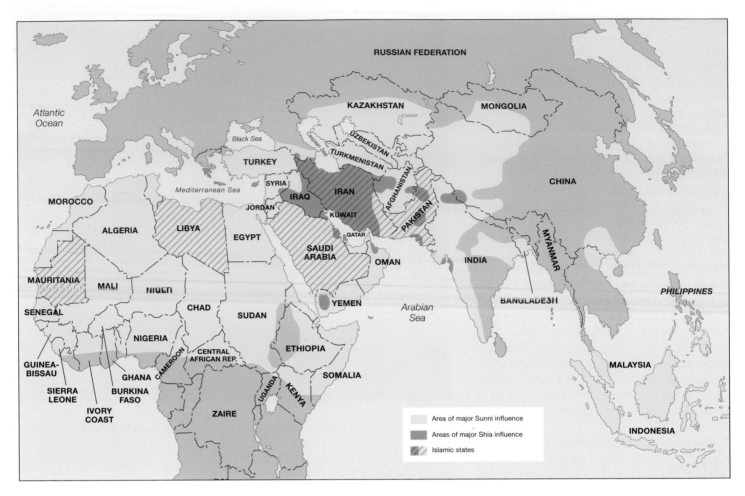

Area of major Sunni influence

Areas of major Shia influence

Islamic states

This map shows the major nations affected by Islamic fundamentalism in the 1980s and 1990s.

tradition. Under President Anwar Sadat (1918–1981), who came to power in 1970, Egypt became closely allied with the United States. The domestic problems this alliance created were compounded by Sadat's own behavior. Traditional Egyptians were outraged, for example, when he appeared on television greeting the wife of U.S. president Jimmy Carter with a kiss on the cheek. To strict Muslims, this was a gesture of indecent intimacy.

Sadat's worst crime in the eyes of many even moderate Muslims was to make peace with Israel. The United States–brokered Camp David accords between Egypt and Israel in 1978, in which Egypt recognized Israel's right to exist, caused Sadat to be hailed in the West as an outstanding statesman and peacemaker. In the Muslim world, both inside and outside Egypt, the peace deal was denounced as a betrayal of the common Arab and Islamic cause.

The Camp David accords came against a background of mounting violence by Islamic extremist groups in Egypt, which bombed Christian churches and carried out attacks on cinemas and other symbols of "ungodliness." On October 6, 1981, militants shot Sadat dead while he was reviewing a military parade. The assassination led to fears that Egypt would witness a repeat

of the events seen in Iran, but Sadat's vice president, Hosni Mubarak, adopted policies almost identical to those of his predecessor. In reply, Islamic terrorists continued their bombings and shootings in Egypt. They targeted Western tourists in an effort to undermine the economy but showed no sign of being able to overthrow the government itself.

## State Terrorism

Terrorism became the preferred tactic of Islamic militants in many countries (*see 9:1238*). Iran and another of the most radical Muslim states, Libya, supported terrorist groups, providing arms and funds for attacks on Western and Israeli targets. The United States denounced what it referred to as "state-sponsored terrorism."

Libya had been ruled since 1969 by the unpredictable Colonel Mu'ammar Gadhafi (b. 1942), who propounded his own brand of revolutionary philosophy and Islamic fundamentalism. Gadhafi used his country's oil wealth to fund an active foreign policy that included sending troops to support the Ugandan dictator Idi Amin in the 1970s (*see 9:1225*). In the 1980s, according to American intelligence, Gadhafi paid for and directed terrorist attacks on American targets. In 1986, after a bomb explosion in a West Berlin discotheque popular with U.S. soldiers, President Ronald Reagan launched air strikes on Libya that nearly killed Gadhafi himself. It is believed that Libyan agents were also responsible for the explosion that destroyed a passenger jet over the Scottish town of Lockerbie in December 1988, killing 270 people.

Shiite terror groups backed by Iran were more active than Libyan groups, particularly in Lebanon, Israel's northern neighbor. Lebanon comprises a patchwork of different ethnic and religious groups. The population was split almost equally between Christians and Muslims, yet each of these factions was itself divided: the Muslims, for example, included Sunnis and Shiites, who were not always on the best of terms with each other.

The situation was further complicated by the presence of refugees from Israeli-occupied Palestine. Their refugee camps were used as bases by the guerrilla fighters of

Refugee camps to house Palestinians were established in southern Lebanon, but they offered only basic living conditions.

A historic moment in Washington, D.C., on March 26, 1979. U.S. president Jimmy Carter (center) witnessed the signing of the Camp David accords by President Anwar Sadat of Egypt (left) and Prime Minister Menachem Begin of Israel.

# Terror and Terrorists

Terrorism in the second half of the twentieth century was a global phenomenon. In Europe, the Red Brigades of Italy kidnapped and murdered the country's prime minister. In Germany, the Baader-Meinhof gang staged shootings and bombings. In Ireland, the Catholic IRA and Protestant terror groups carried out bombing and sectarian assassinations. In Latin America, groups such as Peru's Shining Path killed tourists as part of a campaign against the government. In Africa and Asia, terror campaigns were waged against expatriate communities in the struggle for independence. It was in the service of the Islamic jihad, or holy war, however, that late-twentieth-century terrorism was most employed.

From the end of the 1960s into the 1990s, Islamic fundamentalism inspired a dramatic upsurge in terrorism that led to the deaths of many Muslims and non-Muslims alike. Some Islamic fundamentalists claim that the duty of Muslims to spread Islam through a holy war makes all non-Muslims a legitimate target for attack. In fact, Middle Eastern terrorism is rarely purely religious in its inspiration but also reflects less idealistic political and nationalistic considerations.

The tactics of terrorism vary but the purpose remains the same: to instill fear in the public and thus pressure governments into certain policies. To be successful, terrorism needs publicity. Without media exposure, terrorism can have only a limited effect; terrorists therefore tend to attack high-profile targets. Terrorists realized that the best way to gain the attention of the West—more effectively, for example, than launching raids on Israel—was to attack Westerners. Americans, in particular, were favored targets, partly because the United States was seen as the greatest symbol of Western dominance and partly because an attack on U.S. citizens guaranteed maximum exposure in the media.

There are various sources of Middle Eastern terrorism. Palestinians protesting the loss of territory to Israel found support from Syria, Iran, and Libya, the latter two of which virtually made state sponsorship of terrorism an element of foreign policy. Terror groups bombed indiscriminately, using suicide bombers to attack heavily guarded targets such as foreign embassies or in attacks inside Israel. Other tactics included the hijacking of buses, trains, cruise liners, and aircraft. In Beirut, terrorists kidnapped westerners and held them for years in order to raise the profile of the Palestinian struggle against Israel. Eventually,

The cockpit of a Pan Am Boeing 747 lies in a field near the Scottish town of Lockerbie after the plane was blown out of the sky by a terrorist bomb in 1988. The attack, which killed 270 people, prompted a worldwide increase in airport security. It is thought to have been caused by Libyan terrorists.

The U.S. embassy in Beirut, photographed from a helicopter after a terrorist bomb destroyed much of the building on April 18, 1983.

the hostages were released with few tangible gains by the hostage takers.

In the early 1990s, the occurrence of terrorist attacks decreased as the Middle East stabilized. In countries where radical Muslims still fought for political control, however, terror was not dead. Western tourists found themselves under attack in both Algeria and Egypt as the twentieth century drew near a close.

Photographed by their captors in 1987, four U.S. and British hostages in Beirut hold up a banner to promote the cause of their kidnappers.

Colonel Gadhafi of Libya (left) meets with Egyptian president Hosni Mubarak in a traditional tent outside Cairo in 1999. Gadhafi was seeking to resolve the crisis caused by Libya's apparent role in the Lockerbie bombing of 1988.

Proudly carrying his father's AK-47 assault rifle, an Afghan boy poses for the camera in 1998. The United Nations believes that more than 400,000 children died in Afghanistan's war against Russia and the civil war that followed.

Yasir Arafat's Palestine Liberation Organization (PLO). In 1975, civil war broke out in Lebanon between Muslims and the PLO on one side and Christians on the other. Matters were made worse by outside intervention, first by the Syrian army and then by the Israelis.

## Many Tragedies in Lebanon

In June 1982, Israel launched a full-scale invasion of Lebanon in an effort to crush the PLO. Israeli forces put the Muslim part of the capital, West Beirut, under siege and eventually forced the PLO fighters to withdraw to northern Lebanon, from where they were evacuated to Tunisia. The Israeli triumph was short-lived, however. They allowed their Lebanese Christian allies to carry out a massacre of some 900 civilians in the Palestinian refugee camps of Sabra and Shatilla in West Beirut, losing much international support. Lebanese Shiite terrorists, meanwhile, inspired by Iran and calling themselves Hezbollah—"Party of God"—proved just as dangerous as the PLO. Hezbollah attacked Israeli forces in southern Lebanon and civilian targets in northern Israel.

In 1983, American forces were ordered into Lebanon as part of a multinational force (MNF) attempting to establish a political settlement favorable to Western interests. The Americans presented a tempting target to Hezbollah militants, inspired by Ayatollah Khomeini's call to destroy the Great Satan. On October 23, 1983, two Shiite suicide bombers blew up an MNF barracks, killing 239 American and 58 French military personnel. Western forces were withdrawn soon afterward.

The Iranian-backed Lebanese extremists adopted a new tactic: hostage taking. They kidnapped westerners in Beirut in an effort to put pressure on Western governments. Some hostages were held for five years or more, though all were set free by the end of 1991. At one stage, the United States agreed to sell arms to Iran in return for the release of U.S. hostages. The U.S. government diverted the money it earned to right-wing Contra rebels in Nicaragua. This act led to the Iran Contra scandal that rocked Washington in the mid-1980s (*see 9:1205*).

In another development, the United States decided to support Muslim fighters in Soviet-occupied Afghanistan. In December 1979, the Soviet Union sent troops to help the communist Afghan government combat an uprising among the country's mountain tribes. The Afghani mujahideen, or "holy warriors," were armed by Islamic states, including Iran and Pakistan, and also by the United States, for which the struggle against communism took precedence over confrontation with militant Islam. With such backing, the mujahideen proved a stubborn foe, and the Soviets withdrew their forces from Afghanistan in 1987.

## Fundamentalism in the 1990s

Afghanistan soon descended into civil war, with rival mujahideen warlords fighting for control. In 1996, an Islamic fundamentalist group called the Taleban took control of the capital, Kabul, and declared Afghanistan "a completely Islamic country." They introduced a rigorous Islamic regime that made Iran seem almost liberal. Women were banned from working and forced to wear a full veil in public, a whole range of modern inventions were banned, including television, and harsh punishments were imposed for minor offenses.

In Algeria, the fundamentalist Islamic Salvation Front looked poised to win an

Sheltering from the sun and from the intrusive camera, Iraqi women line up outside a Baghdad mosque for handouts of food in 1997. Following the Gulf War, UN sanctions against Iraq, and the distribution of resources by the Iraqi government, many ordinary citizens were left short of food.

At a 1994 meeting, Israeli prime minister Yitzhak Rabin (left) shakes hands with the Palestinian leader Yasir Arafat. Rabin's efforts to make peace with the Palestinians led to his assassination in 1995 by a Jewish extremist.

election in 1993 but was prevented from taking power by the military government. Islamic militants took their revenge by killing anyone who did not support them, including civilians who had no interest in politics. By 1999, tens of thousands of Algerians had been murdered.

Islamic terrorists continued to target the United States in the 1990s. The bombing of the World Trade Center in New York in February 1993 was the work of a Muslim group, as were the bombings of two U.S. embassies in Africa in 1998. The latter were a response to American missile attacks on Iraq and Sudan. Islamic militants also continued to attack Israel. Lebanese Hezbollah guerrillas fought an intermittent war with Israeli troops in southern Lebanon, while Palestinian Hamas terrorists carried out several bomb attacks in Israeli cities, using suicide bombers to cause maximum casualties.

Such attacks continued in spite of a peace settlement between Israel and the Palestinians. In 1993, Israeli prime minister Yitzhak Rabin and PLO leader Yasir Arafat reached an agreement that would give the Palestinians self-rule in the West Bank and Gaza. For making this accord, Rabin was assassinated by a Jewish extremist in 1995.

In elections held soon afterward, Rabin's Labor Party was defeated, and Benjamin Netanyahu's Likud Party formed a right-wing coalition, which immediately slowed down implementation of the peace settlement. Netanyahu insisted that the peace deal could not go ahead while Hamas attacks continued; Arafat pleaded that such attacks were the actions of individuals and that the best way forward was through the peace settlement already agreed upon.

## Signs of a Retreat

By the 1990s, Islamic fundamentalism was in retreat in Iran, the country where it began. After Ayatollah Khomeini died in 1989, religious leaders who shared his views continued to dominate the country. In 1992, however, the number of mullahs elected to Iran's parliament dropped to 20 percent, compared with 50 percent in 1980.

In 1997, a huge majority of voters elected a moderate cleric, Ayatollah Khatami, president. Hard-line mullahs did all they could to block Khatami's liberalizing reforms, but even so, women began to emerge from repression and play an active role in political life. Iran was on its way to forging a new society that would be neither an imitation of the West nor a return to its strict Muslim past.

# The Postcommunist World

## *The Revival of Nationalism*

Two generations of East Europeans had known no government except communism when, in the late 1980s, economic and political reform swept the region. The reforms unleashed popular protest that within a short time swept away the apparatus of communism, leaving unstable societies. The difficulties of adopting free-market economics led to falling living standards and rising corruption. Nationalist tensions, suppressed under communism, resurfaced. In Yugoslavia, for example, ethnic hatred fanned a decade of civil war.

### The Beginnings of Change

The wave of change was initiated in the Soviet Union. Since World War II, it had dominated the so-called Soviet bloc: Poland, Czechoslovakia, Hungary, East Germany, Bulgaria, and Romania. These countries were linked militarily by the Warsaw Pact and economically by the Council for Mutual Economic Assistance,

or Comecon. Romania was largely independent of Russian influence—like the two communist states outside the Soviet bloc, Yugoslavia and Albania—but the other states remained obedient to Moscow. The Russians supported rulers who governed as virtual dictators but who presented themselves to their own people as a preferable option to direct Soviet rule. The system relied on force. The Red Army crushed a popular rising in Hungary in 1956 and took over Czechoslovakia in 1968.

In March 1985, Mikhail Sergeyevich Gorbachev (b. 1931) became general secretary of the Communist Party of the Soviet Union. Gorbachev faced numerous crises. The Soviet economy was failing, thanks largely to its reliance on inefficient heavy industry, a result of attempts to create a planned economy (*see 7:926*). Over 40 percent of the USSR's hard currency went to importing food. For almost a decade, the economy had remained solvent only

These Soviet pins and medals, once important visual symbols of the communist state, became no more than a collection of souvenirs for sale to tourists after the collapse of the USSR.

1243

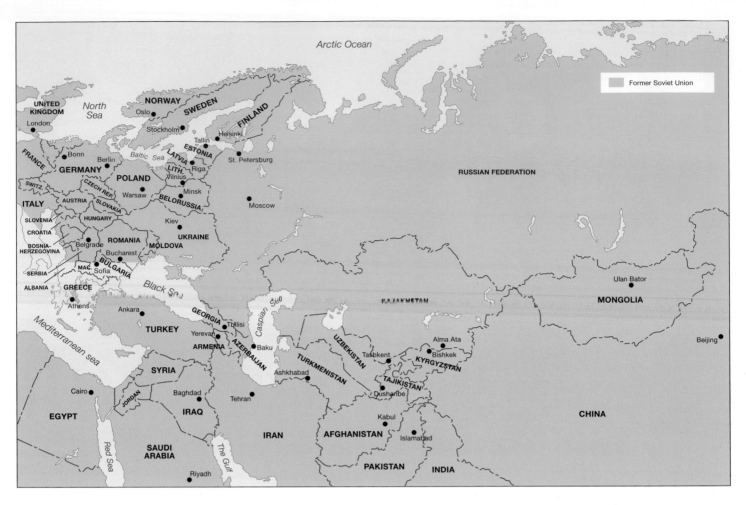

This map shows the states that emerged in the former Soviet Union from 1989 onward.

because of taxes on alcohol, particularly vodka. Since 1980, the Soviet Union had been involved in a costly and unwinnable war in Afghanistan. Influence in Eastern Europe was also expensive: the USSR had to maintain army garrisons in its satellite states and supply their industries with subsidized oil and raw materials.

**Glasnost and Perestroika**
Gorbachev responded to the crisis with policies called in Russian *glasnost*, or "openness," and *perestroika*, or "reconstruction." In a series of measures, he introduced an effective national legislature, removed many old-guard communists from the bureaucracy, released political dissidents, and withdrew Russian troops from Afghanistan in 1989. The explosion of a nuclear reactor at Chernobyl in Ukraine in 1986 highlighted the change in attitudes. Far from following traditional Soviet secrecy, Gorbachev announced the disaster to the world.

Gorbachev was eager to raise investment from the West to underpin economic growth. Partly to encourage good international relations, he announced in April 1985 that the Soviet Union would no longer interfere in the countries of Eastern Europe. The next year, he explained that

"the essence of perestroika…is for people to feel they are the country's master." The governments of the Soviet bloc were abandoned to their fate.

**The Death of Communism**
Some countries of Eastern Europe were better placed than others to take advantage of the Russians' new attitude. In Czechoslovakia, the intellectuals of the Charter 77 group had a long history of protest. It was Poland, however, that had the strongest opposition movement, and it was there that the collapse of communism began.

In 1979, the Solidarity trade union emerged to protect workers in the Lenin Shipyard in Gdansk. It grew into a virtual political party supported by half of a population dissatisfied with economic failure, authoritarian government, and the suppression of Catholicism. In response, communist leader Wojciech Jaruzelski decreed martial law in December 1981 and outlawed Solidarity. The organization did not disappear, however; its leader, Lech Walesa (b. 1943), won the Nobel Peace Prize in 1983. Jaruzelski relaxed military rule gradually, but in 1988 economic reforms provoked widespread strikes. Unable to solve the crisis, the communists held talks with opposition groups and in

Pope John Paul II, himself a Pole, stands beside Polish premier Wojciech Jaruzelski on a 1986 visit to Warsaw. The Pope's visit did much to stimulate antigovernment opposition in Poland.

April 1989 agreed to end one-party rule. Elections produced a coalition government dominated by Solidarity but with communists in key positions. In 1990, Lech Walesa was elected president.

The Poles' efforts to adopt a free-market economy anticipated those of other states. Faced with foreign debt, inflation, and falling production, the government introduced economic controls that led to a fall in the standard of living. In 1990, inflation reached 700 percent, and a tenth of the workforce was unemployed. In elections in October 1991, less than half of Poles voted. Economic suffering had brought a swift disillusionment with democratic freedom. The Polish economy improved through the 1990s, and Poland remained committed to democracy. In 1999, Poland joined NATO, its former enemy, along with two other states that had been in the Warsaw Pact, Hungary and the Czech Republic.

## Reform in Hungary

Hungary had been undergoing cautious reform for twenty years. Communist leader János Kádár (1912–1989), who came to power after the Soviet suppression of the Hungarian revolt in 1956, convinced the Russians to allow him some independence. In 1968, he introduced the New Economic Mechanism, which tried to mix a planned and a free economy. The policy stalled, however, and relied on foreign loans that left Hungary deeper in debt. In 1988, the Communist Party replaced Kádár. Weakened by internal splits, the communists called elections in 1990. They lost to the Hungarian Democratic Forum, which promised gradual transition to a market economy. The elections encouraged nationalism, which threatened to upset relations with neighbors with large Hungarian minorities: Slovakia, Serbia, Romania, and Poland. Nearly one in five Hungarians were ruled by foreign governments.

Hungary was disappointed in its hope that the new central Europe would adopt a system of free borders like that adopted by the European Community in the late 1990s. Instead, it continued to negotiate with its neighbors in an effort to minimize nationalist tensions in the region. Governed from

Mikhail Gorbachev (right) poses with President Ronald Reagan (center) and Vice President George Bush on a visit to New York in 1988.

1994 to 1998 by the Hungarian Socialist Party, made up of reform-minded former communists, Hungary adopted a free market economy. The focus on business brought suffering to many Hungarians but encouraged international investment. For much of the decade, Hungary received a quarter of all Western investment in the former Soviet bloc.

### Change in Czechoslovakia

Governed by the authoritarian Gustáv Husák since the Red Army crushed a pro-democracy movement in the capital, Prague, in 1968, Czechoslovakia was, like its neighbors, in economic crisis. Its out-dated factories polluted the country so badly that it made many Czechs ill.

Opposition to Husák's rule was led by Charter 77, a group of writers and intellectuals formed in 1977 to demand human rights. The group, whose spokesperson was playwright Václav Havel, maintained its demands in the face of police harassment. In November 1989, in reaction to police suppression of a student demonstration in Prague, Havel organized opposition groups into the Civic Forum, aimed at destroying communist rule. When workers launched a national strike, the communist government resigned. A month later, on December 29, 1989, Havel was elected president. The end of communism was so smooth that Czechs called it "the velvet revolution."

Among Havel's problems was the ethnic balance between the nation's two peoples, the Czechs and Slovaks. A strong secessionist movement emerged in Slovakia, where nationalist leaders had by 1992 negotiated the division of Czechoslovakia into the Czech Republic and Slovakia.

### Revolution in Romania

The overthrow of communism was most violent in Romania, where Nicolae Ceausescu had ruled since 1965. Largely independent of the Soviet Union, the dictator was popular with the West. In 1983, then U.S. vice president George Bush called him "one of Europe's good communists." In fact Ceausescu tolerated no opposition, supported a personality cult through a ruthless secret police, the Securitate, and ran the economy with no regard for his people. An urbanization program he launched in the late 1980s, for example, planned to bulldoze half of Romania's villages and replace them with apartment blocks. After his downfall it was revealed that thousands of Romanian orphans were confined in squalid homes.

Romanians were eager for change, and the spark for revolution came in December 1989, when police attempts to deport an ethnic Hungarian pastor in the town of Timisoara led to protests and violence. When the dictator appeared in the capital, Bucharest, he was greeted not with the accustomed applause but with shouts of protest. Protesters were fired on by the army and the Securitate. When protests continued, Ceausescu and his wife fled the city. They were captured and shot by the opposition on Christmas Day.

Ion Iliescu formed a government mainly comprising former communists. There was no democratic tradition in Romania, and Iliescu turned to violence to maintain

Appealing to the economic power the West has over Russia, a protester in the Latvian capital, Riga, urges the withdrawal of all Russian troops from his homeland.

1246

Cut in the shape of a map of Germany, a protester's wooden sign used in demonstrations for the reunification of East and West Germany in late 1989 declares, "We are one people."

power, using gangs of communist miners to beat up and intimidate the opposition. He also fanned nationalism, setting his thugs on Romania's minority Hungarian population. A drive toward a free-market economy led output to fall by more than a half.

In Bulgaria, dictator Todor Zhikov tried to bolster his popularity in summer 1989 by turning on the minority Turkish population, many of whom fled to Turkey. In November 1989, reformers within the Communist Party dismissed Zhikov. In free elections, the communists defeated Western-oriented opposition parties by appealing to nationalism and fear of capitalism. The communist bureaucracy stayed in place, slowing economic reform.

In Albania, revolution against communism came only in 1991. The poorest country in Europe, Albania could barely support itself. Only charitable supplies from Italy prevented mass starvation in the country in 1991. The next year saw the election of Sali Berisla, the first noncommunist president.

## East Germany Goes West
Change in some states inevitably impacted on their neighbors. In September 1989, the Hungarian government allowed migrant East German workers to travel to neighbor-

Georgians applaud a speaker at a pro-independence rally held in the capital, Tbilisi, in 1990 as part of the campaign that led to Georgia's independence that same year.

ing Austria. The decision gave East Germans the chance to defect to the West for the first time since the 1960s.

On October 6, 1989, Mikhail Gorbachev arrived in East Germany to celebrate its fortieth anniversary and warned, "he who comes too late is punished by life," which people saw as an invitation to fight for freedom. The anticommunist demonstrations held on Mondays in Leipzig grew to more than 700,000 strong. Later that month, party leader Erich Honecker was removed from power. On November 9, 1989, the government reopened the border with West Germany, and the Berlin Wall fell. After negotiations with the Allied nations that had occupied Germany after World War II—the United States, the USSR, Britain, and France—Germany was reunified at midnight on October 2, 1990, after forty-five years of political division.

Western politics and economics soon swamped the concerns of East Germany. The elections in March 1991 were a triumph for the Christian Democrats of West Germany, who sold East Germany's assets rather than modernize them. An influx of goods from the West soon adversely affected full-time work and employment in the former East Germany.

## Fragmentation Intensified

As the constituent republics of the USSR adopted elected congresses, glasnost encouraged non-Russians to voice their resentment of Russian and communist influence. In 1986, there were violent protests in the central Asian republic of Kazakhstan against the imposition of a local Russian party chief. The republics were also opposed to each other. Tensions between Armenia and Azerbaijan, for example, flared into violence in the disputed territory of Nagorno-Karabakh.

In the Baltic states, demonstrations against Soviet rule began in Latvia in 1986 and soon spread to neighboring Estonia and Lithuania. The Soviet Politburo tried to suppress a nationalist uprising in Minsk—now capital of Belarus—but the rebels escaped to safety in Lithuania. The central government felt little alarm. The two largest republics, Russia and Ukraine, between them home to 70 percent of the

Created in 1991, these figures from a satirical version of traditional Russian nesting dolls show Boris Yeltsin (center) flanked by two figures of Mikhail Gorbachev.

1248

population, remained quiet. In addition, so many ethnic Russians lived in the rebellious states that the government hoped that any uprisings could be contained.

Nationalism intensified in Ukraine after the disaster at Chernobyl, however. In 1989, Lithuania dropped Russian as the state language. Latvia soon followed suit. In the Georgian capital, Tbilisi, in April 1989, there was a demonstration in favor of national independence. The Soviet Red Army intervened and killed nineteen civilians. In June, Estonia declared economic autonomy, and Lithuania asserted its right to overrule Soviet legislation.

Also in June, there were interethnic riots between Uzbeks and Meshketian Turks in Uzbekistan. Soon there was violence among national groups in Kazakhstan, Tajikistan, and Georgia, where Georgians fought Abkhazians and demonstrated for independence. In August, more than a million people formed a human chain through the three Baltic states to protest the 1939 Nazi-Soviet Pact, which had led to their conquest and incorporation into the USSR.

Determined to preserve the Soviet empire, Gorbachev sent troops to Uzbekistan, Estonia, and Latvia to discourage discontent. He could not use the army everywhere, however. It was expensive and aroused condemnation in the West. Gorbachev had to give ground. The Soviet Communist Party's monopoly of power ended in 1990. No political force was ready to replace the party as a unifying element, further encouraging nationalism. In June 1990, the radical Boris Yeltsin was elected president of the Russian Federation on an anti-Soviet program. By spring 1991, the USSR was on the point of disintegration.

### The Breakup of the Soviet Union

Gorbachev faced greater immediate threats than the breakaway republics. In August 1991, while he was on vacation at the Black Sea, a conspiracy of hard-line communists and military and KGB leaders attempted to overthrow him. With Gorbachev held prisoner, the world held its breath as it seemed that the hard-liners had triumphed. The day after the coup, however, Russian leader Boris Yeltsin climbed onto a tank outside the parliament building in Moscow and urged Muscovites to resist the coup, which was eventually abandoned in the face of popular protest.

The coup left reformers dominant over a weakened Gorbachev. In its aftermath, the Communist Party was outlawed. Independence movements gained strength: Estonia, Latvia, Lithuania, and Moldova resisted orders from Moscow; Kazakhstan also opposed the union, while Turkmenistan demanded independence. In Russia, Yeltsin refused to sign a proposed new Union Treaty. So did Ukraine, which voted for independence on December 1.

Later that month, Russia, Ukraine, and Belarus declared a Commonwealth of Independent States (CIS) to replace the USSR. The Baltic states joined, as did republics from the Caucasus and central Asia. Also disbanded in 1991 was Comecon, whose members urged closer ties with western Europe. On December 25,

Defaced by protesters but also bearing a flower placed by admirers, this statue of Joseph Stalin, Russia's hard-line communist dictator, was resurrected in Moscow's Gorky Park in 1991 by communists unhappy with the dismantling of the Soviet state.

СЫР·МАСЛО
СМЕТАНА

With only a little garden produce to sell, a man and woman sit in a Moscow street in this photograph from 1989. Before and after the collapse of communism, Russia's agricultural output was unable to support the whole population, and food shortages were common.

1991, Gorbachev bowed to the inevitable and stepped down as leader. On December 31, the USSR was abolished.

Boris Yeltsin came to power as the leader of the new Russia in January 1992. He was faced with an immediate choice between calling elections to seek a mandate for radical economic reform and ruling by decree. He chose the latter option, likening himself to Czar Peter the Great (*see 4:486*).

Yeltsin introduced a free market for most goods and made the government give up its right to fix prices. That month, prices rose by 245 percent. Almost the only thing that saved Yeltsin from a popular revolt was the fact that many Russians had amassed savings during the communist years, when there was virtually nothing to buy.

### Problems and Shortages

The transfer to a free-market economy was made more difficult by population movement. Russia was inundated with soldiers returning from military service in the old Soviet empire and later by ethnic Russians fleeing from fighting among the peoples of Tajikistan. The poor flocked to the capital, where tent encampments sprang up in some downtown areas.

Shortages led to the rapid growth of small-scale entrepreneurship. Large sectors of the economy returned to barter. People stole produce and tools from their workplaces to trade with others who had stolen from their employers. The new government made little attempt to restrict such practices. The streets were full of beggars.

Although communism had been abolished, a substantial group of old party members remained, almost all of whom hated Yeltsin. Some of them worked with criminals to promote commercial interests. Political killings became commonplace. Russian generals sold weapons to anyone, even gangsters and terrorists. Individuals exported anything they could, including nuclear fuel and precious metals. Illegal export of Russian diamonds threatened to ruin the world market.

Property and business formerly owned by the state were to be gradually privatized. In 1992, the government introduced a voucher system that allowed each citizen to invest up to 10,000 rubles in new companies, which would all sell 25 percent of their shares. Rapid inflation made 10,000 rubles an insignificant amount, however, and a provision for internal buyouts meant that managers usually bought the businesses in which they worked. Trade unions had little influence, but directors of agricultural, energy, and manufacturing industries formed lobby groups that held great sway over Yeltsin. One of the most influential industrialists was Viktor Chernomyrdin, chairman of the state-owned gas company, who later became prime minister of Russia.

### Economic Failure

As 1992 ended, although food production was only 9 percent down from 1991, government funds were so depleted that the state could not pay farms for produce. Throughout the country, kiosks sprang up from which tradesmen sold imported goods and homemade imitations. With the value of the ruble falling daily, U.S. dollars effectively became Russia's everyday currency.

Just as Russia had wanted to leave the USSR, so parts of Russia now agitated for autonomy. Chechnya, in the Caucasus, declared independence in November 1991, and several other republics now decreed that their own legislation take precedence over decrees from Moscow. In summer 1993, even Yeltsin's home town, Sverdlovsk, declared itself the capital of the short-lived independent Urals Republic.

In 1994, Russian troops entered Chechnya to try to suppress the rebels. The territory was vital to Russia because of an oil pipeline that ran across it from the Black Sea. Years of fighting ruined the Chechen economy and its capital, Grozny, and cost more than 70,000 lives. The long war resolved little, however. The Russians were unable to defeat the Chechens.

Yeltsin looked to the West to provide a fund to help stabilize the Russian economy. The finance did not arrive. The West held back the money because Russia's poverty and the massive state subsidies still granted to the oil and gas industries created an unstable business environment. In March 1993, Yeltsin's opponents began impeachment proceedings against him. Yeltsin held a referendum in which he received a 59 percent majority in favor of his presidency and 53 percent support for his economic policies. Yeltsin dismissed the Supreme Soviet, called elections, and proposed a new constitution. The state assembly would have two chambers, a duma, or parliament, and a council of the federation. Yeltsin fared badly in the resulting elections, however. A weakened position and ill health undermined his presidency through the mid-1990s. In 1998, the ruble collapsed, again draining many Russians of their life savings. At the end of the century, Russia's drive toward the free market remained hampered by its communist past.

## War in Yugoslavia

While the former Soviet Union and Eastern Europe struggled with political and economic reform, the fall of communism had its most dramatic consequences in Yugoslavia. The country, created by the Treaty of Versailles in 1919, was a federation of states of mixed ethnic background and religion. After World War II, communist leader Marshal Tito held together the fractious republics largely by personal authority until his death in 1980. As local communist

Boris Yeltsin, photographed at his desk in May 1988, when he was a member of Mikhail Gorbachev's Soviet government, became president of Russia in 1990.

Ships negotiate their way out of the commercial seaport at Saint Petersburg, once Russia's imperial capital. Following the collapse of the Soviet Union, the port thrived as some Western companies rushed to sell their goods in the new market.

parties and bureaucracies gained in power, financial problems exacerbated tensions between nationalities. Those tensions had deep roots. During World War II, for example, many Croats had supported the Nazis and inflicted barbarous suppression on the Serbs and other peoples. In 1987, the nationalist Slobodan Milosevic took over the largest republic, Serbia. When Slovenia and Croatia declared independence in June 1991, Serbia attacked Croatia, home of a large Serb minority. The Serbs captured the eastern part of the country before agreeing to a truce in spring 1992.

In March 1992, Bosnia-Herzegovina declared independence. Its population included Muslims, Serbs, and Croats, who each began massacring minorities in their regions. Serbia captured areas in the north and east, and local militias drove out Muslims and Croats through intimidation and execution. This "ethnic cleansing" allowed Serbia to consolidate its hold on regions it had captured. The Bosnian capital, Sarajevo, was besieged, and people on all sides died from bombs and snipers.

The wars in Yugoslavia left nearly 250,000 people dead or missing, most of them Muslims, and another three million as penniless refugees. The countries of the West were reluctant to become militarily involved, but the diplomatic and peace-keeping efforts of the United Nations did little to prevent aggression by all sides, particularly the Serbs. In 1999, the West did interfere in the region when Serb attempts to drive the minority Albanian population out of the Serb province of Kosovo led to air strikes on Serbia by NATO forces led by the United States and Britain. The forces unleashed by the fall of communism still threatened to destabilize the whole region.

Symbolic of Russia's new eagerness to embrace modern technology, this photograph from 1997 shows Russian prime minister Victor Chernomyrdin greeting Bill Gates, CEO of Microsoft. Gates was visiting Russia to gain government aid to prevent software piracy.

# The World of Technology

*The Effects and Ethics of Modern Scientific Developments*

In the second half of the nineteenth century, the pace of technological development began to play an increasingly important part in daily lives as new materials and techniques of mass production emerged (*see 6:787*). Change continued through the first half of the twentieth century with the development of automobile, aviation, and communications technologies. Scientific discoveries, and their application through technology, had many positive implications. Advances in medicine helped increase the average human lifespan and relieve suffering. Communications became quicker and more reliable. Alternative forms of energy production promised to overcome problems introduced by the industrial revolution in the early nineteenth century. By the later twentieth century, however, technology played such a large part in every aspect of life that some people began to fear its negative

influence. Nuclear research led to the development of the atom bomb, which cast its shadow over international relations for decades after World War II (*see 8:1059*). New chemical processes, applied on an industrial scale, resulted in enormous problems of waste, pollution, and damage to the environment (*see 9:1263*).

## World War II

Many technological changes had their roots in World War II (1939–1945). The conflict saw governments on both sides invest huge amounts of money in scientific research as they sought to gain an advantage on the battlefield. The resulting advances profoundly influenced not only weapons but also such fields as communications and medicine.

Many experts believe that the war marked a change in the very nature of technology. In 1963, Derek de Solla Price pub-

Symbol of the nuclear age, a mushroom cloud rises above the U.S. desert after an atomic test explosion in the 1950s.

1253

lished his influential book *Little Science, Big Science*. Price argued that World War II hastened a transformation from "little science," restricted to small-scale research, to "big science." Big science brought together large teams, sponsored by governments or private corporations, to collaborate on academic research and the development and application of new scientific techniques. The resulting transformation is sometimes called the Third Industrial Revolution.

## Weapons and Warfare

The immediate results of scientific research in World War II came in arms development. Among the significant advances was a dramatic improvement in the design and power of military aircraft. It had become clear that air supremacy would be crucial to an effective military campaign. Aircraft engines grew more powerful, from 500 horsepower in 1935 to 2,500 horsepower by 1944. The war also hastened the development of the jet engine, which forces air through gas turbines to produce propulsion. The technology had been developed by British scientist Frank Whittle in the 1930s, but the government only provided significant backing for the project once war began and by 1944 jets

Fired from a French submarine, an MSBS M-4 missile rises into the sky during a test in 1985. The nuclear ballistic missile, France's first, had a range of over 2,500 miles (4,000 km).

Photographed in 1995, U.S. Longbow Apache helicopters represented the height of aviation technology. Heavily armed and capable of flying beneath enemy radar, the Apache was an effective rapid-deployment gunship.

were in service with the Royal Air Force. The first jet-powered aircraft had actually made its maiden flight in Germany in 1939.

The jet engine allowed aircraft to fly higher and quicker, greatly contributing to the postwar development of commercial air travel. Equally influential in the postwar world was the wartime development of a system for tracking enemy aircraft, radar. The word is an acronym for "*ra*dio *de*tection *a*nd *r*anging." The British development of radar played a vital role in the airborne Battle of Britain (1940).

Significant military developments in World War II included the introduction of rocket-powered weapons that were the forerunners of sophisticated modern guided missiles. Germany developed the *Vergeltungswaffe*, or "vengeance weapon," a rocket capable of striking over long ranges. The fourteen-ton V-2 could reach an altitude of more than 100 miles (160 km). Members of the V-2 research team went on to play an instrumental role in both the U.S. and Soviet space programs.

A key development was the atomic bomb, developed by the U.S. Manhattan Project and used against the Japanese cities of Hiroshima and Nagasaki in 1945. Driven by the competition between the superpowers, atomic weapons underwent intense development during the Cold War. The fission bombs of 1945, in which energy was released by splitting atoms, were replaced in the early 1950s by more effective fusion bombs, in which energy was released by uniting atomic nuclei. In the 1960s, atomic and rocket technology combined to create intercontinental missiles that allowed powers to threaten each other from thousands of miles away. During the Cold War, the threat of nuclear attack dominated relations between the United States and the Soviet Union, which both invested vast amounts of money in the race to develop better nuclear capability.

Military theory since World War II has stressed the need for high maneuverability. The helicopter has become vital to the rapid deployment of troops. During the Vietnam War (1954–1975), the United States developed the use of the helicopter as a ground-attack gunship. Helicopters played an important part in the Gulf War of 1991, and U.S. Apache helicopter gunships were deployed during the Balkans conflicts of the late 1990s.

Since the emergence of gunpowder weapons and standing armies in the fifteenth century, the ability to wage war has relied on economic as much as military strength. Modern military technology is astronomically expensive. The Strategic Defense Initiative, known as SDI or Star Wars, was a U.S. research program intended to provide an antiballistic-missile defense system. Launched by President Ronald Reagan in 1983, it would have used new weapons, including high-powered lasers and particle beams fired from satellites in space. Soviet attempts to match SDI went a long way toward bankrupting the communist system in eastern Europe, while even in the world's richest country, SDI proved too expensive and was cut back in 1991.

The world's most sophisticated military aircraft at the end of the century, the B-2 stealth bomber. With a range of nearly 10,000 miles and designed to be nearly invisible to enemy radar, the stealth bomber became a central weapon in the U.S. military arsenal.

1255

With astronaut Neil Armstrong reflected in his visor, Edwin "Buzz" Aldrin walks on the moon during the 1969 *Apollo 11* mission. Armstrong was actually the first human to set foot on the moon.

## The Space Race

German wartime research into rockets laid the foundations of the Soviet and U.S. space programs. Space exploration aroused intense opposition from people who argued that the expenditure of vast resources on putting astronauts into space was a waste of money. The earlier stages of the space programs, however, were largely prompted by the realization of the benefits of placing satellites in orbit above the earth. Such satellites had wide applications in telecommunications, meteorology, geology, and military reconnaissance.

In 1957, the USSR launched *Sputnik I*, the first artificial satellite. The launch precipitated what became known as the space race, as the USSR and the United States competed to gain an advantage. Following a successful earth orbit by Soviet cosmonaut Yuri Gagarin in 1961, U.S. president Kennedy launched the Apollo program, aiming to achieve a piloted lunar landing by 1970. An unmanned Soviet Luna mission landed on the moon in 1966 but in 1969, Americans Neil Armstrong and Edwin "Buzz" Aldrin became the first persons to set foot on the lunar surface.

A TV audience of millions worldwide watched the moon landing, but the achievement marked the height of the popularity of the space program. During the 1970s, more and more people came to question the investment necessary as both the United States and the Soviet Union launched long-term space stations. In 1981, the United States launched the first reusable space shuttle, intended to reduce the cost of deploying and repairing satellites. The program was temporarily interrupted five years later when the shuttle *Challenger* exploded shortly after lift off.

## Looking into Space

Among the various payloads carried by the resumed space shuttle program was the Hubble Space Telescope (HST), deployed in 1990, which crystallized attitudes toward space exploration. Above the distorting effects of the earth's atmosphere, the HST achieves surpassingly clear images of distant solar systems. Critics who argued that

The 1975 docking between a U.S. Apollo spacecraft and a Soviet Soyuz capsule, commemorated by this shoulder patch with the astronauts' names, marked a significant improvement in relations between the two countries.

such images are of little practical use were bolstered by the fact that an error in one of Hubble's mirrors meant that the telescope was of only limited use for five years until it was repaired by a later shuttle mission. Supporters of space exploration argue that Hubble images will reveal information about the creation of the universe and, ultimately, about the creation of Earth and the nature of human life. Further accurate information about the solar system came from the interplanetary probes of the Mariner, Venera, Pioneer, and Voyager series.

The space race also had various practical technological by-products. Water filters in many homes rely on technology developed to provide clean water for astronauts. Cordless machines such as drills and shrub trimmers were developed by NASA in conjunction with the U.S. corporation Black and Decker. Satellites enable live TV broadcasts to be relayed around the world. Aluminum and ceramic heat shields designed to protect spacecraft have prompted the development of improved methods of home insulation. Even space

Photographed on July 4, 1995, the U.S. space shuttle *Atlantis*, at bottom, is connected to the Soviet space station *Mir*. The shuttle delivered a new crew to the space station and flew the previous crew home.

1257

A technician checks connections on the giant ENIAC computer at the U.S. Army base at Aberdeen, Maryland, in 1947. ENIAC weighed 30 tons and incorporated 18,000 vacuum tubes.

A model's finger tip shows the tiny scale of an Intel computer microprocessor, a complete electronic circuit on a silicon chip. This chip was photographed in 1982.

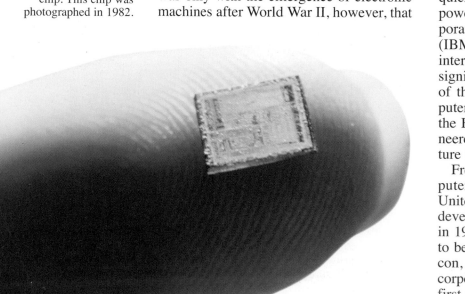

suit technology has practical applications, providing sealed outfits for sick children susceptible to infection.

## The Computer Age

If one technological innovation came to dominate the late twentieth century, it was the computer. As its name suggests, the computer was originally a relatively simple calculating device for computation, or math, though it soon evolved into a sophisticated data storage and retrieval system. A prototype digital calculating machine was actually devised as early as the 1830s by English mathematician Charles Babbage. It was only with the emergence of electronic machines after World War II, however, that computers began the rapid spread that characterized the late twentieth century. Personal computers became common in offices, homes, and schools. Computer technology changed aspects of life from supermarket checkouts to car design, from magazine printing to TV sports analysis. The world market for computers was well in excess of $200 billion by the beginning of the 1990s, a remarkable achievement for an industry that barely existed at the end of World War II.

As computers developed, their potential for a wide range of industrial, administrative, and scientific applications became rapidly apparent. The earliest computers were huge machines, often as big as a room. They included ENIAC, the Electronic Numerical Integrator and Computer, used mainly for military purposes; EDVAC, the Electronic Discrete Variable Computer, the first computer to store a program in its memory; and UNIVAC, or Universal Automatic computers, used for a variety of commercial purposes.

Computers' application remained limited until their miniaturization was made possible by the invention of the transistor by John Bardeen, Walter Brattain, and William Shockley at Bell Telephone Laboratories in 1947. The transistor, a tiny device used to regulate the flow of electric current, lies at the heart of modern electronics. It enabled the miniaturization of established products such as cameras, televisions, and radios.

The first transistor-operated computer was built at Manchester University, England, in 1953, and the United States quickly developed a number of much more powerful computers. In 1954, the U.S. corporation International Business Machines (IBM) developed FORTRAN, the first international computer language. Another significant development was the creation of the world's first mainframe supercomputer, Atlas, by Manchester University and the British Ferranti corporation. Atlas pioneered many aspects of computer architecture that remain common.

From the mid-1950s, most major computer developments took place in the United States. Particularly crucial was the development of the integrated circuit (IC) in 1958, which allowed a complete circuit to be manufactured on a tiny piece of silicon, often called a chip. In 1972, the U.S. corporation Intel developed the world's first microprocessor, the Intel 4004, which was directly responsible for the development of today's cheap, fast, and reliable personal computers. Further refinements in

PCs continued with the addition of video displays and larger storage devices. First developed by the U.S. corporation Xerox, graphical user interfaces (GUIs) were used by Apple Computers, Inc., to produce the Apple Mac.

Modern operating systems such as Windows 98 and Linux have evolved to enable users to run a huge diversity of programs and manipulate remarkable amounts of data. The rapid evolution of the computer has also led to an increase in abuse. Computer hackers illegally access systems, often with damaging results: viruses and worms can spread from computer to computer, deleting or changing essential files and causing system failures. In the workplace, using computer hardware has led to an increase in conditions such as Repetitive Strain Injury (RSI) and may contribute to raised levels of stress among workers.

## The Development of the Internet

A significant development in computing was the emergence of the Internet, which evolved from a computer network at the U.S. Advanced Research Projects Agency, or ARPA, in the 1960s. The initial experimental network, ARPANet, linked computers at Stanford Research Institute,

California, with University of California campuses at Los Angeles and Santa Barbara and the University of Utah.

Throughout the 1970s, an increasing number of universities and institutions joined ARPANet, sharing information with each other. Its users soon found it necessary to set up a protocol—or code of conventions—to standardize transmissions of data. The result was Transmission Control Protocol, or TCP, and the Internet Protocol, or IP, the foundations of international Internet communication.

As various administrations, scientific organizations, and academic groups developed their own communication networks, ARPANet developed into the Internet. British computing expert Timothy Berners-Lee made the Internet easier and more efficient for people to use with the introduction of the World Wide Web (WWW). The Web dramatically increased the usefulness of the Internet as a research, commercial, and leisure resource. The graphic interfaces of the WWW were especially useful for viewing multimedia files containing text, sound, graphics, video streams, and animation. As Internet applications become more sophisticated and as its popularity increases, the massive amount of informa-

Young people experiment with the Internet in London's Cyberia Internet café in this photograph taken in the 1990s. Internet cafés became increasingly popular as the World Wide Web made the Internet itself more accessible for ordinary users.

tion will require new technologies. The Internet also faces problems—such as the regulation of pornographic or criminal material—that need to be solved by legislation or technological development.

## Transportation and Communications

Late-twentieth-century developments in transportation largely continued prewar trends. The automobile, train, and ocean liner saw few changes to their basic design. The airplane, however, has seen a remarkable growth in popularity, due mainly to the introduction of jet propulsion as a consequence of wartime military development. Transatlantic passenger flights began soon after the end of World War II, and huge jet-propelled civilian airplanes evolved to meet demand, at the cost of increasingly crowded airways and noise pollution. A civilian supersonic plane that flies faster than the speed of sound, the British-French Concorde, came into service in the 1970s.

One remarkable development in post-1945 transportation was the invention of the air-cushion vehicle (ACV). ACVs, or hovercraft, ride on a cushion of air without touching the surface over which they travel. The hovercraft is remarkably versatile, but its further development seems unlikely given the popularity of existing forms of transport.

While existing forms of transport remain popular, the fossil fuels, such as gasoline, on which they depend create pollution and threaten eventually to run out. Such concerns have spurred research into alternative power sources; electric vehicles may become more popular. Japan has pioneered research into magnetic levitation, or maglev, technology, a high-speed ground transportation system in which a vehicle levitates above a track called a guideway and is propelled by magnetic fields. Many other nations have investigated this clean and energy-efficient system.

Leaning on his restored 1930 Citroen, a Vietnamese businessman from Ho Chi Minh City (formerly Saigon) talks on his mobile phone. Advances in communications technology saw mobile phones become highly popular in developing countries as well as in the industrialized West.

1260

Photographed in a laboratory in Australia, optical fiber cable such as this provides a reliable, high-speed medium for transferring telephonic and digital information.

## Telecommunications

Telecommunications changed remarkably quickly after World War II. Of particular importance were the rapid growth of television broadcasting and its impact on domestic societies as a medium of mass communication. Television also played an influential role in globalization, the process by which the world's countries grew increasing interconnected and culture increasingly uniform (*see 9:1276*). The development of digital rather than analog technology and of the satellite network orbiting earth promoted the rise of global television networks. Since their inception in the 1960s, satellites have also played an important role in fields from telecommunications to meteorology, relaying data around the world.

Communications also benefited from other areas of research. For example, the laser (*l*ight *a*mplification by *s*timulated *e*mission of *r*adiation), first developed as a weapon, can provide a high-power light beam for long-distance communication.

A final innovation in communications technology was the use of electromagnetic radiation rather than light to explore the

The Anglo-French Concorde, the world's first supersonic passenger airliner, has a top speed of 1,354 miles an hour, or over Mach 2.

The computer has proved a powerful tool for medical research and imaging. Computed axial tomography (CAT), positron emission tomography (PET), and nuclear magnetic resonance (NMR) all provide detailed images of the inside of the human body. Photographed in 1992, this doctor in Grand Rapids, Michigan, is examining 3-D X rays of a skull and brain.

universe. The radio telescope and its X-ray counterpart are vital instruments in space research and satellite control. Radio telescopes are also being used in the search for signals from intelligent life forms in the universe. Radio waves remain only partly understood by science, however. The boom in mobile phones in the 1980s and 1990s, for example, led to serious concerns about a possible link between the phones and brain tumors.

## High-Tech Medicine

World War II provided the stimulus for significant medical research, particularly in pharmaceuticals. The antibiotic properties of penicillin were essentially a wartime discovery, developed in secrecy by the United States and reserved for military use. Not until the late 1940s did penicillin become available for civilians.

Surgical technology improved dramatically after the war, particularly techniques for organ transplantation. In 1967, South African surgeon Christiaan Barnard carried out the first heart transplant. Liver, kidney, and lung transplants have also been successfully performed. Doctors have also successfully reconnected severed hands and limbs using microsurgery to connect tiny severed nerves.

Postwar medicine was characterized by the use of statistics. The causative link between smoking and lung cancer, for example, was discovered from largely statistical evidence published in a 1960 report by the American Heart Association. Medicine was also marked by reference to a new discipline, molecular biology, which was spurred on by the 1953 discovery by Francis Crick, James Watson, and Rosalind Franklin of the structure of deoxyribonucleic acid (DNA), the genetic basis of replication and human life. Molecular biology underlay research into fields such as fertility, biotechnology, and genetic engineering. It enabled, for example, the cloning of a sheep, Dolly, by British scientists in 1997.

The cloning of Dolly, like early transplantation experiments that placed animal organs in human hosts, raised many ethical questions for the medical profession. The use of biotechnology to genetically modify crops was equally controversial. Scientists are interfering with the natural order of the world, argue critics. Such has been the speed of scientific development since 1945 that scientists threatened to leave public support behind. For many people, the unrestrained advance of technology became a reason for concern rather than celebration.

# The Natural World

*Nearing the Limits of Sustainable Growth*

By the late twentieth century, rapid population growth and 200 years of industrialization were placing unprecedented pressure on the earth's natural resources. As a result, many people became increasingly aware of the potential problems facing humankind. Individuals and governments agreed that steps had to be taken to avert disaster. Many problems seemed too severe to solve, however. For others, resolution would demand far-reaching changes in individual behavior.

### Early Warning Signs

The industrialization of Western countries from the early nineteenth century brought clear signs of possible damage to the natural world. Towns and cities grew rapidly; domestic and industrial waste turned rivers and canals vivid colors and killed aquatic life. Smoke darkened the air as world coal consumption rose forty-six-fold. Leaves withered on trees. In Britain, a species of moth turned dark to disguise itself more effectively against soot-covered surfaces.

Economic prosperity and technological achievement, however, tempted contemporaries to turn a blind eye to industry's impact on the natural world. The dominant philosophy of the age was a belief in human supremacy over nature. A few voices protested. The U.S. writer Henry David Thoreau (1817–1862), author of *Walden, or Life in the Woods* (1854), argued that humans must live in harmony with nature and that nature rather than economic progress underlay prosperity. Thoreau's warnings were timely: much of the American landscape was being turned over to provide timber, minerals, and other resources for industry. The conflict between the needs of industry and those of nature would become more pronounced in the twentieth century.

Garbage surrounds a bulldozer in this photograph taken in 1990 at Reclamation Island, a U.S. garbage dump. At such dumps, refuse is compacted and covered with a layer of soil, allowing the site to be used for other purposes. Many major cities, however, are running out of space for landfill sites.

A packed beach in Gijón, Spain, photographed in the 1980s, gives a vivid impression of how much more crowded the world is becoming. The earth's population doubled in only thirty years in the second half of the twentieth century.

would eventually limit the population by starvation or the effects of sickness on ill-nourished people. What Malthus did not predict, however, was the twentieth-century advent of genetic modification and other techniques intended to expand the earth's capacity to produce food.

## An Early Warning
Developments in farming sometimes have serious side effects, however. A clear warning of the consequences of intensive farming came in the United States, where the growing population saw uncultivated areas brought under the plow. From about the end of World War I in 1918, the Great Plains of western Kansas, Oklahoma, and northern Texas were settled by so-called sodbusters, farmers who turned the grassy plains into wheat fields to cash in on rising food prices. Before the sodbusters planted single-crop fields, the plains had supported a complex variety of grasses.

Throughout the 1920s, the farmers thrived. Disaster struck in 1931; for the next five years, not enough rain fell and the wheat crops failed. The plains' naturally drought-resistant grasses had been wiped out, and as the soil grew drier, there were no roots to hold it in place. The whole region became a dust bowl (see 7:968). Desperate farmers turned to soil experts, who advised them to reintroduce more varied vegetation. Failure fully to follow the advice led to further crises in the mid-1950s and again in the mid-1970s.

The dust bowl was a stark warning of the potential consequences of increasing agricultural yield. For most of history, natural resources—soil, water, forests, plants, and animals—replaced themselves at a natural rate. In the twentieth century, farmers increasingly relied on chemical pesticides and fertilizers to destroy pests and enhance growth, respectively, speeding up natural processes. Intensively farmed animals raised in confined spaces became subject to disease and were given antibiotics, which became so widely used that they lost much of their efficacy, leading to still higher dosages. The result was the introduction of artificial chemicals into the food chain, the potential long-term effects of which remain little understood.

## The Green Revolution
Following the end of World War II in 1945 and the decolonization of much of Asia and Africa, the United Nations took the lead in introducing new methods of farming in the developing world. The so-called green revolution aimed to meet the demand for

## Population Growth
At the root of humankind's shifting relationship with the planet was a remarkable rate of population growth. Between 1850 and 1930, the number of people on earth doubled from one to two billion. Despite national initiatives to limit birth rates, it more than doubled again to reach 5.3 billion by 1991. Some predictions believe that the global population will peak in 2045 at just under eight billion.

The rate of population growth increases as the number of people on the earth grows. Growing national populations could cause increasing conflicts over land and water, accelerate the speed at which the planet's resources are used up, and increase starvation and poverty. In the late eighteenth century, the English biologist Thomas Malthus (1766–1834) predicted that lack of food increased food production by using chemicals, machinery, and new crops and animals. The green revolution has nothing to do with the later green movement. UN-sponsored initiatives were successful in parts of Asia: India doubled its production of wheat in fifteen years, and the rice crop in the Philippines rose by 75 percent. The initial success soon vanished, however. Many farmers could not afford the large quantities of chemicals they needed. The overall effect of the green revolution was to make farming increasingly expensive, and thus to widen the gap between rich and poor farmers in the developing world.

Some farming initiatives did succeed, such as the cultivation of the soybean in east Asia, particularly in Japan and China. Originally grown for animal feed, the soybean proved a cheap source of protein as bean curd, cooking oil, and soy milk. Its use spread to the West, particularly as a popular protein substitute for vegetarians.

## The Silent Spring

One of the most influential critics of new farming techniques was U.S. biologist and writer Rachel Carson (1907–1964). Carson argued the importance of maintaining the balance between humankind and nature. Her most famous book, *Silent Spring*, published in 1962, alerted the public to the dangers of synthetic pesticides, particularly DDT. Such pesticides, Carson argued, entered the food chain, and as animals were consumed by others, the poison became more concentrated. Carson's nightmare world was silent because no birds remained alive to sing. Partly in response to Carson's campaign, the U.S. government largely banned the use of DDT in 1972. Carson's work profoundly influenced the later ecology movements of the 1970s and 1980s.

## Lessons of the Amazon

Human impact on the natural world is intimately connected not only with demographics and food supply but also with global economics. The gap between the world's rich and poor countries, or between the developed and the undeveloped world, forces poorer countries to overexploit their natural resources, often by selling them to the industries of the developed world. Such trade can have serious consequences, as in the Amazon region of Brazil.

The demand for rubber in U.S. industry in the early twentieth century stimulated outside companies to exploit the Amazon's rubber plantations. Indigenous rubber tappers had learned to plant trees a hundred yards apart. This distance provided the

A crop-duster airplane sprays a wheat field with pesticide in this photograph taken in North Dakota in the 1980s.

Author Rachel Carson in 1963, the year after she published *Silent Spring*. Carson was once employed as a biologist by the U.S. Fish and Wildlife Service.

Latex drips from grooves cut into a rubber tree in Malaysia. Rubber production depends on elementary methods of tapping natural resources. Efforts to intensify the process led to disaster in the Amazon in the early twentieth century.

This aerial shot of a part of the Amazon rain forest shows the results of slash-and-burn farming, by which farmers clear forest to provide land for farming.

plants with light and nutrients and quarantined them against the spread of disease. In an effort to maximize profits, the newcomers planted trees much closer together. The results were catastrophic. Disease spread rapidly, and the industry failed.

The Amazon, whose rain forest is one of the most ecologically diverse and valuable habitats on earth, became a potent symbol of the interaction between humans and the natural world. The threats to the region's biological balance crystallized many of the debates within the conservation movement.

The most prominent threat to the Amazon is deforestation. The rate at which the world's trees were cut down accelerated in the second half of the twentieth century. In the 1990s alone, 4 percent of all tropical forests were felled. Half the loss occurred in just seven countries: Bolivia, Brazil, Mexico, and Venezuela in the Americas, the Democratic Republic of the Congo (formerly Zaire) in Africa, and the Southeast Asian nations of Indonesia and Malaysia. Deforestation on such a scale had global implications. Trees absorb carbon dioxide and produce oxygen, and scientists believe that the loss of trees—by increasing the amount of carbon dioxide in the atmosphere, which traps the sun's heat— contributes to global warming.

The economic and political issues surrounding deforestation are complex. Some who urged protection of forests drew a simplistic equation between global impact and Western commerce. They urged measures such as consumer boycotts of furniture made from rare hardwoods. While it might be desirable to regulate commercial lumber operations, they are not the only cause of deforestation. In many poorer countries, forests are felled to provide farm land for peasants who are themselves usually the poorest people of a nation. It is difficult for well-intentioned campaigners to deny such people land they need or to condemn a state for seeking to feed its population. Many developed nations underwent similar large-scale felling of forests to create arable farm land many centuries ago.

In the 1960s, Brazil's military government decided that the Amazon region was an underused national resource. It began a policy of relocating poor farmers from the country's fertile plains to Amazonia in order to create more arable land. The farmers cleared land using the slash-and-burn technique: they cut down the trees, burned the vegetation, and used the cleared land to cultivate crops. Similar techniques are common wherever a predominantly poor population lives in forested regions, as in Southeast Asia. Slash-and-burn is an effective short-term form of agriculture, because the ash fertilizes the land. Such land soon becomes exhausted, however, and farmers need to clear new land. Indigenous forest peoples found their habitat destroyed by loggers and relocated peasants. In Amazonia, organized resistance by indigenous Indian populations led to violent clashes and murder. The stakes were high. One scheme to exploit Amazonia, the Grande Carajas project, will affect an area the size of Britain and France combined, creating plantations, ranches, mines, hydroelectric dams, and heavy industry.

## The Problem of Pollution
As human beings labored to make the planet as productive as possible, they also made it dirtier. The nature of pollution has changed. Before 1945, it was mainly caused by the burning of fossil fuels, such as coal and oil, and the production of iron and steel. After World War II, the chief sources of pollution were toxic synthetic chemicals that were resistant to degradation by natural processes. The use of detergent instead of soap in washing powder, for example, dramatically increased phosphate levels in U.S. domestic water supplies. Toxic pesticides, although they affected all aspects of life, did not even reduce crop loss. In the United States, the share of the harvest lost to disease between the 1940s and 1980s increased, from 32 to 37 percent.

Pollution has also become increasingly a political issue. Air and water pollution respect no political boundaries, so contamination caused by one nation can easily affect its neighbors. Contamination from the nuclear explosion at Chernobyl, in Ukraine, in 1986, for example, spread over much of northern Europe. Efforts to control pollution, too, need global coordination, which creates difficulties. Developing nations are often unable to afford the more efficient technology necessary to reduce pollution. Such nations argue that, by imposing pollution targets, the developed world is unfairly hampering efforts at modernization and economic development.

Debates about pollution create other conflicts and dilemmas, too, even on a local level. People who want to buy manufactured goods might still object to living next to the factory that produces them because of the pollution it creates.

## Global Warming
A potentially damaging result of pollution is global warming. Many scientists believe the average temperature in the atmosphere is increasing, largely due to the buildup of carbon dioxide, which traps heat. Rising

A child of the Kayapo people of the Amazon. The rain forest is still home to many Indian peoples, some of whom practice hunter-gatherer lifestyles. Attempts by the forest's indigenous peoples to resist external incursions were met by violence on the part of lumber companies and settlers.

A rescue worker cradles a bird covered in oil during the cleanup of Prince William Sound, Alaska, after the Exxon Valdez oil spill in 1989. More than 250,000 birds died as a result of the disaster.

temperatures have various effects. The world's deserts are spreading. As the polar ice caps melt, rising sea levels threaten coastal dwellers, often the poor. Low-lying countries, such as Bangladesh, in Asia, risk flooding and saltwater infiltration while islands, such as the Maldives in the Indian Ocean, may eventually be submerged.

The first warning of global warming came from a Swedish scientist, Svante Arrhenius, as early as 1896, when burning fossil fuels had already released measurable carbon dioxide into the atmosphere. The release of carbon dioxide increased dramatically after the 1950s, rising about 19 percent in thirty years, mainly as a result of increased vehicle exhaust emissions. Almost half of carbon-dioxide emissions come from just eight countries, of which the United States is the largest contributor, with 17 percent of the global total.

Scientists debate the causes and extent of global warming. Some point out that the atmosphere is highly complex, that statistics of rising temperatures may be unreliable, and that relatively warm periods may have affected the planet in the past. The complex computer simulations that predict climate change suggest that, if global warming does occur, it might be uneven. Such simulations, however, can only partially predict the variety or interaction of factors that might either increase or lessen the effect of global warming.

## El Niño and Climate Change

The effects associated with global warming can also be partly explained by natural phenomena, such as El Niño. El Niño is a regular disruption of weather patterns in the Pacific. It was given its Spanish name, "the Christ Child," in the nineteenth century by fishermen in Chile who noticed an unusual warm offshore current around Christmas. El Niño's alterations in ocean and air currents have been blamed for many extreme weather conditions. In 1982 and 1983, for example, the strongest El Niño on record coincided with Australia's worst-ever drought and torrential storms throughout the American Southwest.

Other climatic changes serve as a reminder that humans remain in many ways as dependent on the vagaries of nature as in previous centuries. Drought affected some parts of Africa in the 1980s. Three failed harvests in a row devastated Ethiopia, for example. Countries and aid organizations have food supplies to cope with the worst effects of famine, but those effects were often worsened by human actions. In Ethiopia, civil war prevented food from reaching hungry people, and disease from insanitary refugee camps killed more people than actual hunger.

## Managing the Oceans

One of El Niño's most profound effects has been the disruption of the seasonal anchovy harvest off the coast of Chile and Peru, damaging food supplies. Humans also continue to use oceans, rivers, and lakes as dumping grounds for urban garbage and industrial chemicals. In 1956, an outbreak of fatal mercury poisoning among fishing families in Minamata, Japan, was traced to the buildup in shellfish of toxic mercury discharged from a local factory.

Pollution was sometimes traceable to accidents. Bulk tankers were often poorly maintained and managed. In March 1989, the oil tanker *Exxon Valdez* ran aground in Prince William Sound in Alaska. Eleven million gallons of crude oil escaped, polluting thousands of miles of coastline. The disaster killed 250,000 seabirds, at least 1,000 rare sea otters, and many other animals. An expensive cleanup operation took years to restore the sound's ecology.

Overfishing drastically reduced some fish species as commercial net fishing resulted in a massive decline in the world's fish stocks. Established food fish, such as cod, became rare and were replaced by deep-sea species, such as angler and monkfish. By the late twentieth century, quotas limited catches around the world and set standard minimum sizes for net mesh, so that nets allowed baby fish to escape so that they could mature and breed.

### Threats to the Atmosphere

Two centuries of fossil-fuel burning and other industrial processes have had a damaging effect on the atmosphere. Although much of the developed world now limits atmospheric emissions, the same is not always true of countries that are eager to catch up economically. Global warming is only one potential result of pollution. The vehicle exhausts that may contribute to global warming are major causes of the smog that hangs over many of the world's cities. Pollution also causes the phenomenon known as acid rain. Raindrops accumulate particles of substances released into the atmosphere and become acidic. The resulting rain strips foliage from trees.

Extensive pine forests in northern Europe, for example, have been badly damaged by acid rain whose pollutants often originated from the ill-regulated industries of the former Soviet bloc.

A different form of pollution was caused by gases called chlorofluorocarbons, or CFCs, which were widely used in refrigerators, solvents, and aerosols. Released into the atmosphere, CFCs are a major cause of the depletion of the ozone layer in the stratosphere, which serves to reflect many damaging rays of the sun. Its depletion allows more ultraviolet rays to reach the planet's surface, resulting in increased incidences of skin cancer.

### The Challenge for the Future

Some environmental dangers are of humans' own making. In 1979, radioactive gas nearly escaped from the nuclear plant at Three Mile Island, Pennsylvania. In 1986, at the Chernobyl nuclear reactor in Ukraine in the former Soviet Union, radioactive waste escaped into the atmosphere, leaving 3,860 square miles unfit for human use. The radiation drifted, irradiating plants and animals over a wide area. Some 21,000 Europeans were expected to

Smog lies above the city of Los Angeles in this photograph taken at 9:00 A.M. Caused mainly by vehicle exhausts, smog was largely responsible for significant increases in the occurrence of respiratory diseases in many countries, particularly among children.

A worker checks radiation levels at the grave of a victim of the nuclear explosion at Chernobyl in 1986. The explosion caused thirty immediate deaths and afflicted 200 people with radiation sickness.

die of cancer as a result. In Bhopal, India, in 1984, toxic chemicals leaked from a plant into a slum area, killing and disfiguring thousands of people.

## What Is Being Done?

The twentieth century saw an increased awareness of human impact on the natural world. Many individuals began to take steps to minimize that impact. They recycled bottles, tins, and paper, bought produce grown using only organic pesticides, and avoided overpackaged produce. People preferred free-range eggs laid by chickens kept in open spaces as opposed to battery farms, where they are crowded into tiny cages. Where possible, many people walked, cycled, or used public transport instead of their cars.

Consumer pressure affected industry, where many companies went "green" in responses to customer demand. CFCs, for example, were often dropped by industry before they were actually banned by governments. Industry remains a major source of pollution, however, particularly in the developing world. Anomalies still abound. Many parents who believe in conservation continue to use convenient disposable diapers, even though they are not biodegradable.

This pine forest in the Czech Republic has been killed by the effects of acid rain. Sulfuric and nitric acids are formed in the atmosphere by smoke produced by burning fossil fuels.

## The Environmental Movement

Individual efforts both support and are coordinated by numerous campaigning groups that emerged in the last three decades of the century. The best-known is probably Greenpeace, formed in 1971 by people protesting U.S. nuclear weapon testing on Amchitka Island in the North Pacific. Greenpeace uses high-profile, nonviolent confrontation to expose global environmental problems.

Various political parties, called green parties, emerged in many countries to argue for ecological policies. The greens made large strides in Europe in the early 1990s. In the 1996 U.S. presidential election, the veteran consumer campaigner Ralph Nader stood as candidate for the American Green Party. He spent less than $5,000 on his campaign and polled 682,000 votes.

## The Rio Earth Summit

Political leaders responded to their electors' increased interest in the environment with the first world "earth summit" in Brazil, in 1992. World leaders met at Rio de Janiero to address environmental problems. More than 150 nations agreed to reduce or stop emissions of greenhouse gases—gases associated with global warming—to protect and restore natural habitats, and to fund sustainable development. In addition, governments adopted Agenda 21, some 2,000 recommendations on a wide range of environmental, social, and economic issues. Few countries translated the program into significant policy changes, however.

The Rio summit was followed five years later by another in Kyoto, Japan, that underlined the difficulties of compliance. Emissions had risen, particularly in industrializing nations such as China, Brazil, and Indonesia, where they rose by 20 percent since 1990. Emissions also rose in the United States. Claims were made that more than 100,000 plant and animal species became extinct in the five years between the two summits. Each year the world lost forest equivalent to the area of Louisiana.

## The Medical Challenge

The failure of the earth summits is a reminder of the continuing difficulties facing humanity (*see 9:1273*). Some of the hardest challenges come in the field of medicine. The World Health Organization, a branch of the United Nations, was set up in 1948 to organize international efforts to improve health. Campaigns have improved sanitation in developing countries, helping combat diseases such as cholera and yellow fever. In 1980, smallpox was eradicated.

Other diseases remained potentially fatal. Virulent strains of malaria threatened

Trash and recycling bins, like these photographed at an Earth Day demonstration in the United States in 1990, became an increasingly familiar sight toward the end of the century.

Southeast Asia and elsewhere in the developing world. In 1972, a new virus, Ebola, appeared in Sudan, Africa. In 1976 and 1977, outbreaks of Ebola killed hundreds of people in Sudan and Zaire.

The most potentially disastrous new disease was AIDS, or acquired immunodeficiency syndrome. First identified in 1981, the disease is associated with the human immunodeficiency virus (HIV), which is blamed for reducing the body's ability to resist infection. AIDS originated in Africa but spread to other continents. When it spread to the developed world, the disease initially concentrated in homosexual men and drug users but later spread throughout several other groups. In Africa, from 10 to 20 percent of the continent's entire population may be infected with HIV. Strong drugs can for a time retard the effects of AIDS, but it remains fatal. The only way to prevent the spread of the disease is by behavior modification and protection of the blood supply.

## A Positive View

As in most human dealings with the natural world, the power to limit the impact of AIDS lies with people alone. For some commentators, this is the best reason for optimism about humanity's dealings with the planet. They argue against the doomsday scenario that sees humankind rushing to destroy the planet and itself. Optimists suggest that simple awareness of the problems facing the earth—population growth, pollution, global warming, the shortage of resources, disease, and so on—will inevitably stimulate effective responses. Birth control can limit the population, monitoring and investment can reduce pollution and moderate the effects of global warming, sustainable resources can be developed and managed, and science will eventually overcome AIDS, as it has overcome many other diseases in the past 200 years. Some charities argue that the problem is not a shortage of food in the world, for example, but its distribution, which lies within human capacity to sort out.

This attitude is reminiscent of the nineteenth-century belief in human supremacy over nature. Its adherents argue that there is a difference, however. Unlike previous generations, they claim, contemporary humans have such an appreciation of the fragility of the earth that they will not fall into the complacency of their forebears.

Despite warnings about humanity's harmful effects on the planet, some commentators believe that people are better off than at any other time. Fewer people go hungry or die of treatable diseases, while more are able to read and acquire knowledge that allows them to exercise influence over their world. Many people are better off in material terms, too, but judging wealth in terms of money or possessions imposes the values of a consumer society on cultures that might have rejected them. Material wealth also highlights the wide gulf that remains between the rich and poor nations of the world. However humankind might cope with its problems, a more equitable distribution of the world's resources will likely lie at the heart of the solution.

U.S. vice president Al Gore shares a stage with Brazilian Indian leaders during the earth summit held in Rio in 1992. The United States, like most other countries, was largely unsuccessful in translating the rhetoric of the summit into practical action to limit pollution.

# Problems for the Twenty-first Century

*Possible Histories of Tomorrow*

As the twentieth century drew to a close, the people of the world faced challenges as daunting as any that had faced their predecessors at the end of the fifteenth, sixteenth, seventeenth, eighteenth, or nineteenth century. What was unusual about the late twentieth century was the comparative absence of any large-scale ideological or political conflict. At the end of the fifteenth century, for example, warfare was clearly imminent between an expanding Ottoman Empire and its European and Persian neighbors. At the end of the eighteenth century, ideological splits pitted revolution, liberalism, and nationalism against the conservative elements of European society. At the end of the nineteenth century, tensions on a global scale emerged as great powers struggled for world dominance. The twentieth century witnessed extremes of political and ideological conflict, particularly during World War II. The collapse of communism in the Soviet Union and eastern Europe after 1989, however, and the acceptance of the utility of free markets by the largest remaining communist state, China, suggested that capitalist democracy would become the dominant global political and economic system. This system was rivaled by religious and social fundamentalism of various kinds, but fundamentalism did not present a direct threat to the free market in most parts of the world.

The suddenness of the triumph of capitalist democracy was something of a shock.

Warfare and pollution, two of the world's great problems, combine in this image of burning oil wells in Kuwait in 1991. The wells were set afire by defeated Iraqi troops during the Gulf War. The smoke and oil they discharged threatened to devastate the fragile ecology of the Persian Gulf region.

One historian claimed that the new era was "the end of history," because so much of modern history had been dictated by ideological conflicts that were now finished. There are, however, numerous unresolved political problems around the globe that will combine unpredictably with more general social, envinromental, or commercial developments. In a broad sense, the reaction of politicians and thinkers to the new wave of challenges may be difficult to predict. The men and women running the world were brought up in a landscape of intense ideological confrontation and now have to operate in unfamiliar territory.

The problems facing humanity fell into various categories. Many were political, social, or religious. Among the most pressing, however, were environmental concerns (*see 9:1263*). Humankind continued to place great demands on the earth and its resources. The search for alternative technologies and sustainable or renewable resources became more pressing. Despite efforts at regulation, activities such as overfishing and deforestation continued. Between 1975 and 1986, for example, settlers and commercial logging companies destroyed more than 100,000 square miles of rain forest in regions such as Amazonia in South America and Malaysia in Asia. Some scientists argue that the loss of rain forests, which absorb carbon dioxide and produce oxygen, may contribute to global warming. Although not all scientists agree, many believe that growing concentrations of carbon dioxide and other greenhouse gases trap heat in

A sign at Tirana airport welcomes passengers to Albania with an advertisement for Coca-Cola. Such a sign is evidence of the importance of globalization: Albania, Europe's poorest country, had until 1992 a hard-line communist government opposed to the free-market capitalism represented by the U.S. soft drinks giant.

Smoke billows from chimneys at a steelworks in Ukraine in the 1980s. Former Soviet bloc countries found it prohibitively expensive to modernize their industries to avoid pollution.

the atmosphere, causing the average temperature to rise; 1990 was the warmest year on record.

## Controlling the Population

At the root of most environmental problems lay a population explosion. The world population has grown exponentially. In 1750, it stood at about 800 million; in about 1800 it rose above a billion for the first time. The rate of growth increased so rapidly that world population reached two billion by 1930, three by 1960, four by 1974, and five billion in the late 1980s. The total was expected to reach eight billion by 2025. The highest birthrates were in the undeveloped world, in those countries that were least economically and agriculturally able to support population growth. Family planning measures had some success in slowing the growth. China's population exceeded one billion even with strict government limits allowing only one child per family or two for rural families. India, whose population stood at 960 million in 1999, was poised to overtake China as the world's most populous nation because it had no compulsory birth control. In Indian states such as Kerala, where women were better educated, birthrates were much lower.

Population growth increased the demand for food. Human efforts to exploit the natural world sometimes had negative consequences. The use of chemical fertilizers, genetically modified crops, and large-scale farming, for example, came under critical scrutiny. In Britain, a small but significant number of people died from CJD (Creuz Jakob Disease), a human form of bovine spongiform encephalopathy (BSE), sometimes called mad cow disease. BSE was apparently caused by feeding animal carcasses to cows, which are naturally herbivorous, and the disease was passed on to humans in infected meat. The sale of British beef was widely banned. In Guatemala and other developing countries, where chemical controls are not stringent, the overuse of pesticides led to birth defects, blindness, and deformity.

In some parts of the world, particularly in Africa, famine remained a threat that could be triggered by weather conditions such as drought. More often than not, how-

Chinese cyclists crowd a street in Beijing. Compulsory birth control has slowed China's population growth so successfully that India appears destined to overtake it as the world's most populous nation.

A great scourge of the modern age, the AIDS virus remained incurable at the end of the twentieth century. This false-color electron micrograph shows the virus budding through the membrane of a blood cell.

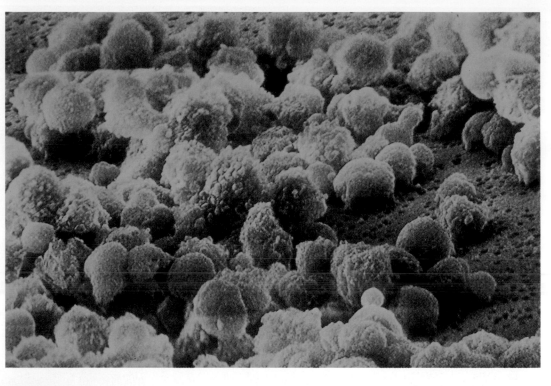

Victim of a crisis she cannot understand, this girl was photographed during a famine in Somalia in 1992. The effects of famine were worsened by civil war in the country.

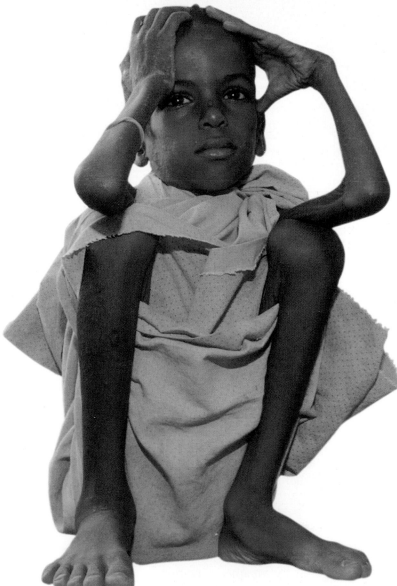

ever, the consequences of famine were worsened by political considerations. In North Korea in the late 1990s, for example, when successive droughts led to crop failure, the mass starvation that followed was exacerbated by the communist government's refusal to accept aid from the capitalist world.

## Globalization and Localization

Many of the world's political problems resulted from the tension between globalization and nationalism. The world became increasingly globalized during the twentieth century. Globalization as a broad term describes how communications and economics, in particular, operate without regard for national borders. Effective worldwide communications meant that popular music or TV programs had a worldwide audience and that brands such as Levi jeans or Sony electronics were known in every country. Large corporations owned subsidiaries in many nations and could move assets around at will. Large companies organized their operations on a multinational level in order to exploit preferential economic conditions across the world. U.S. companies, Reebok for example, built factories in South and Southeast Asia, where labor costs were cheap.

The consequences of globalization are profound. On the one hand, it allowed the economies of countries such as South Korea, Hong Kong, Thailand, and Indonesia to grow rapidly (*see 9:1209*). On the other, it led to job losses in the developed world, where the manufacturing sector inevitably lost much of its importance as factories either relocated or closed in the face of competition from cheaper plants.

A significant result of economic globalization was to make national economies more vulnerable than ever before to short-term economic crises elsewhere. When recession hit Japan in the late 1990s, for example, the effect was felt around the world, spreading first to Southeast Asia but then to Australia and even Brazil. While Europe struggled to avoid the recession, only the U.S. economy continued to expand. Some observers found such expansion ironic, because Japan's recession had itself been caused partly by the rising value of the U.S. dollar.

Economic globalization was enabled by advances in communications and information technology. Computers made it possible to send information anywhere in seconds, making the world effectively a smaller place. British airline companies, for example, employed workers in India to take bookings when their home offices closed. When rebels in the Mexican state of Chiapas began a guerrilla revolt against the government, they popularized their cause on their own web site. The Internet linked the world's scholars and journalists more closely than at any time before.

Culture itself became globalized. Satellite television made it possible for people around the world to watch the same TV programs. North American shows, bands, and sports teams became popular everywhere. The English soccer club Manchester United had more fans in India than in England. Symbols of U.S. consumer brands such as Coca-Cola, MTV, and Microsoft were recognized around the world. Vietnam, for example, experienced vigorous advertising campaigns by Coca-Cola and Pepsi in the 1980s and 1990s. At Hanoi airport, Pepsi-sponsored buses picked up new arrivals and drove them past a giant Coca-Cola billboard.

Some people worried that global corporations exploited the undeveloped world. Nestlé was criticized for selling powdered baby milk to mothers in Africa by pressuring some of the world's poorest citizens to pay money for something they did not actually need. Nestlé, critics said, falsely implied that its product was better for babies than breast milk. Cigarette manufacturers also attracted criticism when, faced with legal constraints in the developed world, they targeted advertising campaigns at teenagers or children in places such as Southeast Asia, where controls were not so strict.

## Economic Disparity

One of the problems of globalization was that it did little to address the fundamental disparity between the world's richest and poorest countries. Indeed, it often widened the gap. While Western corporations exploited economic conditions to grow richer, developing countries attempting to compete for global trade borrowed money for investment and found themselves with crippling debts to the developed world.

The collapse of the Soviet Union in 1991 left the United States as the world's only political and economic superpower. The U.S. economy boomed at the end of the twentieth century while many other countries, including Japan, found themselves in recession. Even within the United States, distinct economic inequality remained. Some inner cities remained impoverished and scarred by drug problems. The same was true in affluent western Europe. Geneva, Switzerland, for example, enjoys one of the highest standards of living in the world but also has a large drug problem.

A road built by loggers runs through the heart of a forest in Sumatra, Indonesia. Although Western organizations protest against deforestation, lumber remains commercially vital for many developing countries, and forest clearance provides much-needed farmland.

The drug problems of the developed world are intimately connected with the poverty of the nations in which drugs are usually produced. The world's poorest citizens remain mired in a daily struggle for food and shelter, living largely hand-to-mouth existences. For some, the drug trade offers a highly attractive way to make a living. Farmers in Bolivia and elsewhere continue to plant coca leaves, from which cocaine is made, despite its being illegal since 1988. Coca is the only cash crop that earns sufficient money for them to live. Attempts to control the drug problem in the developed world have to address the poverty that underlies the trade.

International debt dates back to the late nineteenth century when the newly industrialized countries started to invest in foreign countries. Debt became a problem in the 1970s when an oil crisis led to a world economic slump and the inability of many poorer countries to repay their debts. Many countries rescheduled, or reorganized, their debt by postponing payment of the principal. Countries such as Mexico and Brazil use up more than 50 percent of their exports to repay their debts, which leads to continual rescheduling and nervousness in the world financial markets. Some debtor nations, particularly in Africa, have such high debts that all their surplus national income is spent on debt repayment rather than the provision of even basic health care or education. Campaigning organizations in the developed world tried to urge governments to cancel debts.

## Nationalism

The growing importance of globalization was accompanied by something that seemed to contradict it. Nationalist sentiment was often at least partly a reaction to globalization and the loss of influence some people felt over their own political destiny. Nationalism easily spilled over into ethnic or racist hatred. The Ku Klux Klan still exists in some parts of the United States, and extremist Nazi and fascist political parties win support in some European and Latin American countries.

Nationalist sentiments informed many of the conflicts of the late twentieth century, which were localized rather than global. Many wars had roots in long-established ethnic or religious enmity. In Africa and Asia, the independent nations that emerged after decolonization often split along sectarian lines and descended into civil war or conflict with their immediate neighbors. The disintegration of the Soviet Union in 1991 and that of Yugoslavia both unleashed bitter nationalist struggles rooted in ethnicity (*see 9:1251*).

When the Yugoslav president Marshal Tito died in 1980, the country he had united and ruled divided into independent states. In the 1990s, the region sank into violence as Serbia struggled for domination against Croatia and Bosnia. Serb tactics to clear territory for settlement in Bosnia and the Serbian region of Kosovo introduced a new phrase to the language, ethnic cleansing.

Mass murder, or genocide, was neither new nor limited to Europe. In Rwanda, Africa, differences between the minority ruling Tutsi ethnic group and the Hutu majority spilled over into full-scale civil war (*see 9:1230*). Slaughter and famine virtually destroyed the country. Other parts of the world were also split by violence. India and Pakistan were involved in a long armed struggle over the disputed border province of Jammu and Kashmir, claimed by both countries since partition in 1947 (*see 8:1116*). Civil war racked African countries such as Sudan, Congo, and Angola. Arab nations remained in a state of hostility with Israel.

Crying as she carries what belongings she can, this Muslim woman was fleeing from a Serb attack in Bosnia in 1992. Serb tactics aimed to drive Muslims from certain areas, a policy they termed "ethnic cleansing."

## The Role of Religion

Another common source of domestic and international conflict was religion. Religious differences underlay the conflict between Hindu India and Muslim Pakistan and the terrorist campaigns in Northern Ireland. Religious belief appeared to polarize across the world. Broadly speaking, *fundamentalism* means a strict adherence to the basic principles of faith. Christian fundamentalism thus believes in the literal truth of the Bible, while Islamic fundamentalism adheres to the truth of the Koran and a traditional system of laws. Christian fundamentalists, particularly in the United States, sometimes refuse to recognize earthly authority in the form of government, claiming to obey only God's spiritual authority. Such a rejection of government power sometimes allies fundamentalists with groups such as survivalists and far-right militias that claim the right to replace society's rules with their own.

Like Christianity, Islam is a widely varied faith, and fundamentalists remain a small minority of all Muslims. Where fundamentalism has grown, it has often been a reaction against what is seen as unwanted influence or interference by the West. In countries such as Iraq, Iran, Libya, and Afghanistan, fundamentalism has often been associated with hatred of the Western world, particularly the United States. The Islamic faith also provided a rallying point for Arab campaigns against Israel, particularly after the humiliation of Arab defeat in the 1967 Six-Day War. Religious and political aims came together in the concept of the *jihad*, a holy war against unbelievers, which lay behind terror campaigns within the Middle East and Europe.

Religious and political terrorism was a characteristic of the late twentieth century

(*see 9:1238*). Bombings and murders were common in some countries. The Irish Republican Army, or IRA, killed opponents in Ireland and Britain; Basque separatists maintained a campaign against the Spanish government to establish their own state. Although these European conflicts died

U.S. tanks and vehicles wait to go into action in the Gulf War in 1991. While some people praised the war as an example of international cooperation to defeat an act of aggression, others argued that the Western alliance was motivated only by the desire to protect valuable oil wells.

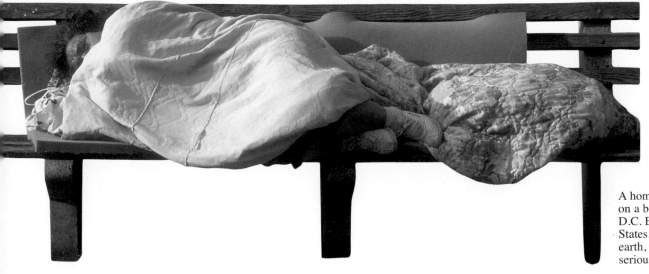

A homeless woman sleeps on a bench in Washington, D.C. Even in the United States, the richest nation on earth, poverty remains a serious social problem.

1279

# The Case for Optimism

Although humanity sometimes seems to face overwhelming problems, the coming of the twenty-first century brought a number of reasons to be optimistic about the future. Even if a significant portion of the world's population still lives in destitution, a much larger share than at any time in the past has the opportunity to achieve greater prosperity.

Causes for optimism existed on both international and local levels. In international relations, multinational organizations attempted with more or less success to prevent conflict, arbitrate disputes, and protect their members. Such organizations included the United Nations, the North Atlantic Treaty Organization (NATO), the Organization of American States (OAS), the European Union (EU), and the Organization of African Unity (OAU). On a local level, public opposition to terrorism was a key motivating factor in the emergence of a proposed peace settlement in Northern Ireland. In Argentina, the weekly demonstrations in Buenos Aires by the mothers of the "disappeared" eventually forced the government to reveal details of the so-called dirty war of the 1970s and 1980s in which their offspring died. In Indonesia, prodemocracy demonstrations forced the resignation of the long-time authoritarian president Suharto in May 1998.

The United Nations was set up in the aftermath of World War II to prevent future wars and coordinate the rebuilding of devastated regions. Its various programs and agencies have been highly effective in improving living conditions in many countries. The World Health Organization eradicated the disease smallpox in 1980. The United Nations Children's Fund (UNICEF) provides health care and education for children in some of the world's least developed countries. The Educational, Scientific and Cultural Organization (UNESCO) promotes international collaboration, but con-

These food supplies have been unloaded from a USAF airplane at Mombasa in Kenya en route to relieve the effects of famine in Sudan in 1991. International agencies, governments, and charities became experienced at mobilizing funds and supplies to cope with such emergencies.

cerns about its cost caused the United States and Britain to withdraw in the 1980s. The High Commission for Refugees (UNHCR) provides temporary shelter and coordinates food supplies for refugees fleeing natural disaster or war. UN peacekeeping troops are sometimes used as a neutral force to halt fighting in or between different countries.

One of the most potent causes for optimism was the changing situation in South Africa, which successfully made the transition from white-minority rule to a government incorporating the black population that for decades had been excluded from the political process by the policy of apartheid. In April 1994, some 28 million black Africans received the vote for the first time.

South Africa overwhelmingly elected Nelson Mandela president. In an attempt to forge a new beginning for the country, Mandela set up in 1996 the Truth and Reconciliation Commission. The commission heard evidence about the apartheid era from secret police, politicians, torturers, and their victims in televised sessions. An amnesty was granted to those who testified for all political crimes, including murder. By confronting the past in public sessions, the commission sought to exorcise the evils of racial acts committed by both whites and blacks. Such an approach differed greatly from that evident in Cambodia, where more than 1.5 million Cambodians were killed by the Khmer Rouge government of Pol Pot from 1975 to 1978. After the Khmer Rouge were toppled by Vietnamese troops and replaced by a nominally democratic government, Cambodians decided not to punish their former governors but to try to leave the past behind. Pol Pot died in 1998 without having stood trial.

The example of South Africa gave cause for hope as it addressed its problems of poverty, discrimination, and hatred. Nelson Mandela himself delivered a message of hope when he proclaimed: "No one is born hating another person because of the color of his skin, or his background, or his religion. People must learn to hate, and if they can learn to hate, they can be taught to love, for love comes more naturally to the human heart than its opposite."

A Chinese mother and her child shop in a supermarket in Guangzhou in 1996. In many parts of the world, rising standards of living brought choice and comfort to a greater number of people.

down near the end of the century, a Singhalese separatist movement in Sri Lanka led to many deaths. The United States was free of terrorism until New York's World Trade Center was bombed by Middle Eastern extremists in 1993. More shocking for Americans was the bombing of the federal building in Oklahoma City in April 1995, when 168 people were killed by American separatists who rejected federal authority.

## The Twenty-first Century

Predicting the future is difficult. History is full of examples of unlikely alliances, falls from power, and unforeseen victories. Few people in 1900, for example, could have predicted that France and Britain would fight together against Germany in 1914. The two were close to going to war with one another over their colonies in Africa. Germany, meanwhile, was Britain's traditional ally, sharing a common ethnic descent and related rulers.

The conflicts at the end of the twentieth century show every sign of continuing. In some countries, warfare is virtually endemic. The African state of Sudan, for example, had only eleven years of peace in the last four decades of the century.

While specific events are impossible to foretell, it is possible to identify general trends. There is evidence, for example, that international bodies, particularly the United Nations, will prevent the escalation and spread of local conflicts. The continued development of weapons and the acquisition by more countries of atomic weapons, however, make even a localized war potentially devastating for the planet.

In terms of the environment, the population will continue to place a great burden on the planet. Despite increased awareness of Earth's fragility, humankind will go on damaging its home. Poor countries often do not have the luxury of choice. They fell trees because they need more agricultural land; factories have no emissions controls because they are too expensive to install.

The spread of globalization looks set to continue, linking the world's countries ever more tightly. If such links are not to cause severe problems, the richest nations need to address the discrepancy with the poorest for the global economy to become stable. Advances in technology, particularly computing, have created an intellectual global village where people can communicate with strangers across the world. The exchange of ideas broadens horizons and breaks down cultural barriers. By inspiring a new vision of the world, it offers a note of hope for the twenty-first century.

The ruins of the federal building in Oklahoma City, after it was blown up by a bomb in 1995, in the United States' worst experience of terrorism.

# Time Line

| EUROPE | AFRICA AND ASIA | THE AMERICAS |
|---|---|---|
| | | **1945** United Nations founded, with headquarters in New York |
| **1946** British prime minister Winston Churchill speaks of a future "United States of Europe" | | **1946** Juan Perón becomes president of Argentina |
| | **1947** India and Pakistan gain independence from Britain | **1947** Transistor invented at Bell Telephone Laboratories |
| **1948** Soviet forces blockade Berlin: Berlin air lift begins | **1948** Creation of state of Israel. South African National Party formalizes policy of apartheid. Syngman Rhee comes to power in South Korea. World Health Organization (WHO) set up to fight disease in developing countries. | **1948** Organization of American States (OAS) founded |
| | **1949** Communists take power in mainland China; Kuomintang establishes Nationalist republican government on Taiwan | **1949** Women gain right to vote in Argentina |
| **1950** Mao Tse-tung visits Moscow: treaty of friendship signed between China and USSR | **1950** Korean War begins. Pass laws established in South Africa. | **1950** Joseph McCarthy begins "witch-hunts" for communists in United States |
| **1951** Treaty of Paris establishes European Coal and Steel Community | | **1951** Jacobo Arbenz elected president of Guatemala with communist support |
| | **1952** U.S. occupation of Japan ends | **1952** Populist revolution in Bolivia. Death of Eva Perón in Argentina. |
| **1953** Francis Crick, James Watson, and Rosalind Franklin discover structure of DNA | **1953** Korean War ends. Chinese begin first five-year plan. | |
| | **1954** Japanese economy recovers to prewar level | **1954** CIA destabilization of Guatemala; elected president replaced by military government. IBM develops FORTRAN, first international computer language. |
| | | **1955** Bus boycott by black people begins in Montgomery, Alabama. James Dean appears in the movie *Rebel Without A Cause*. |
| **1956** USSR crushes popular rising in Hungary and installs Josef Kádár as Hungarian leader | **1956** Rift between China and USSR. after Khrushchev denounces Stalin. Criticism of government and freedom of speech officially encouraged in China. Sudan gains independence; guerrilla war begins in south. Outbreak of mercury poisoning from marine pollution in Minamata, Japan. | |

Timeline markers: 1945, 1950, 1955

20th Century

| EUROPE | AFRICA AND ASIA | THE AMERICAS |
|---|---|---|
| **1957** Treaty of Rome establishes European Economic Community (EEC). USSR launches first artificial satellite, *Sputnik I*. | **1957** Clampdown on freedom of speech in China. Vietnam War begins between South Vietnamese army and Viet Cong guerrillas. Ghana gains independence from Britain. | **1957** First black march on Washington; Martin Luther King calls for end to voting restrictions. U.S. author Jack Kerouac publishes *On the Road*. |
| **1958** Charles de Gaulle becomes president of France | **1958** Mao announces Great Leap Forward | **1958** In Cuba, dictator Fulgencio Batista overthrown by guerrillas led by Fidel Castro. U.S. researchers develop integrated circuit. |
| | **1959** Mao resigns as chairman of Chinese central government council. Rift between China and USSR deepens. | |
| **1960** | **1960** Police kill rioters against pass laws at Sharpeville in South Africa. Mass protests force resignation of South Korean ruler Syngman Rhee. Kwame Nkrumah declares himself president-for-life of Ghana. Congo gains independence from Belgium; Katanga and South Kasai provinces try to break away. | **1960** Cuban missile crisis. Contraceptive pill licensed for sale in the United States. New city of Brasilia becomes capital of Brazil. |
| **1961** Soviet cosmonaut Yuri Gagarin makes first space orbit of Earth. Britain applies for membership of the EEC. | **1961** Park Chung Hee comes to power in South Korea | **1961** Bay of Pigs: abortive invasion of Cuba by U.S.-based anticommunist exiles, with CIA backing |
| | **1962** Mao comes out of retirement to launch a new "socialist education movement" in China. Border war between India and China. Nelson Mandela imprisoned in South Africa. | **1962** Sandinista National Liberation Front formed in Nicaragua. U.S. biologist Rachel Carson publishes *The Silent Spring*. |
| **1963** Charles de Gaulle vetoes British membership of the EEC | **1963** Organization for African Unity (OAU) founded. Kenya gains independence from Britain. Iranian authorities suppress anti-government demonstrations. | **1963** Martin Luther King makes the speech "I Have a Dream." U.S. president John F. Kennedy assassinated; Lyndon Johnson succeeds him. U.S. author Betty Friedan publishes *The Feminine Mystique*. |
| | **1964** China explodes its first atomic bomb. Nelson Mandela sentenced to life imprisonment in South Africa. Ayatollah Khomenei leaves Iran to go into exile in Europe. | **1964** Lyndon Johnson launches "Great Society" program. U.S Congress passes Civil Rights Bill. Warren Commission concludes that Lee Harvey Oswald acted alone in the assassination of President Kennedy. Bob Dylan records "The Times They Are A-Changin'." |
| **1965** Nicolae Ceausescu becomes ruler of Romania | **1965** Massacres of Chinese population in Indonesia. Singapore secedes from Malaysian Federation. Military coups in Nigeria, Congo, and Burundi; General Mobutu takes power in Congo (renamed Zaire). White government of Rhodesia unilaterally declares independence from Britain. | **1965** Race riots in Los Angeles. U.S. Congress ends many restrictions on black Americans' right to vote. U.S. Immigration Reform Act passed. U.S. Marines intervene in Dominican Republic to suppress a popular reformist rebellion. |

**1960**

**1965**

20th Century

| EUROPE | AFRICA AND ASIA | THE AMERICAS |
|---|---|---|
| **1966** Unmanned Soviet space mission lands on moon | **1966** Mao Tse-tung launches the Great Proletarian Cultural Revolution in China. Nkrumah overthrown by military coup in Ghana. Military coups in Central African Republic, Upper Volta (later renamed Burkina Faso), and in Nigeria, where the coup sparks a massacre of Ibos in north. | **1966** Former movie star Ronald Reagan elected governor of California. National Organization for Women (NOW) founded in United States. U.S. author Susan Sontag publishes *Against Interpretation*. |
| **1967** British Labour government legalizes abortion and decriminalizes homosexuality. President De Gaulle repeats his veto of British membership of the EEC. | **1967** Israel defeats Arab neighbors in Six-Day War. In China, Mao calls out army to take back control from Red Guards and restore order. Sukarno displaced as leader of Indonesia. Katangan revolt in Zaire ends. Nigerian civil war begins when province of Biafra claims independence. Christiaan Barnard performs world's first heart transplant. | **1967** Race riots in Newark, New Jersey, and Detroit |
| **1968** Paris students and sympathizers demonstrate against de Gaulle's government; police suppression results in a wave of strikes. "Prague Spring," a movement to liberalize communist rule in Czechoslovakia, suppressed by Soviet army. Hungarian communist government proposes to adopt a mixed economy. | **1968** Liu Shao-chi falls from position of power in China | **1968** Democratic Party Convention in Chicago: antiwar protests result in fighting between demonstrators and police. Martin Luther King and Robert Kennedy assassinated. Republican Richard Nixon elected U.S. president. General Velasco Alvarado seizes power in Peru. |
| **1969** De Gaulle falls from power in France. British government makes divorce easier and permanently abolishes capital punishment for murder. | **1969** Cultural Revolution in China officially declared over. Mu'ammar Gadhafi comes to power in Libya. | **1969** U.S. astronauts land on the moon. Woodstock rock festival. Homosexuals in U.S. begin to campaign against discrimination. |
| | **1970** Anwar Sadat becomes president of Egypt, replacing Nasser. Surrender of Biafra ends Nigerian civil war. | **1970** Four students killed when National Guardsmen open fire on anti-Vietnam protestors at Kent State University. Marxist Salvador Allende elected president of Chile. |
| **1971** Britain reapplies for membership of the EEC | **1971** Lin Biao killed in China. U.S. president Richard Nixon allows China to join United Nations. Idi Amin seizes power in Uganda. | **1971** Greenpeace founded in Canada |
| **1972** Referendum in Norway rejects membership of the EEC | **1972** Nixon visits China; many trade and travel restrictions between United States and China lifted. Ebola virus appears in Sudan, Africa. Famine in Ethiopia, continuing into 1973. Hutus massacred by Tutsi government in Burundi. | **1972** Watergate break-in. Intel develops world's first microprocessor. U.S. government bans use of DDT. |
| **1973** Britain, Denmark, and Ireland join the EEC | **1973** Rapid rise in world oil prices begins. Stock market crash in Hong Kong. Major famine in Ethiopia. | **1973** U.S. Supreme Court ruling gives women the right to abortion. CIA backs right-wing military uprising against President Allende in Chile. |

**1970—**

20th Century

| EUROPE | AFRICA AND ASIA | THE AMERICAS |
|---|---|---|
| **1974** End of postwar economic boom in the Western world brings rapid inflation and mass unemployment. Strikes in Britain bring down Conservative government; Labour Party wins election. Military coup in Portugal brings left-wing army officers to power. | **1974** Emperor Haile Selassie of Ethiopia overthrown, replaced by left-wing military junta. Riots against apartheid in Soweto township in South Africa. | **1974** Resignation of U.S. president Richard Nixon. Augusto Pinochet becomes military dictator of Chile. |
| **1975** Referendum in Britain confirms membership of the EEC | **1975** Vietnam War ends. Communist regimes established in Vietnam, Laos, and Cambodia. Angola and Mozambique gain independence from Portugal. Cuban troops fight on procommunist side in Angolan civil war. Civil war begins in Lebanon, with Muslims and PLO fighting Christians. | |
| **1976** Concorde, the world's first supersonic airliner, goes into service | **1976** Death of Mao Tse-tung. Ebola outbreak in Sudan. | **1976** Milton Friedman wins Nobel Prize for Economics |
| **1977** Human rights group Charter 77 formed in Czechoslovakia | **1977** Eritrea and Ogaden begin fight for independence from Ethiopia | **1977** United States resumes capital punishment |
| | **1978** Deng Xiaoping emerges as new leader of China. Religious students in Iran killed by police during antigovernment protest. Camp David agreement between Egypt and Israel. | |
| **1979** Margaret Thatcher becomes British prime minister. Solidarity trade union emerges in Poland. | **1979** Revolution in Iran: shah flees country, Ayatollah Khomenei takes power and imposes fundamentalist regime. Militants storm U.S. embassy in Tehran and take 52 hostages. Shiite extremists occupy the Great Mosque in Mecca. Saddam Hussein becomes president of Iraq. Vietnamese invasion of Cambodia ends Pol Pot's regime. In China, Deng Xiaoping gives approval to democracy wall movement. Assassination of General Park Chung Hee, leader of South Korea. USSR sends troops to Afghanistan to support communist government against Islamic mountain tribes. Tanzanian invasion force ends Idi Amin's rule in Uganda. White government of Rhodesia forced to accept democratic elections. | **1979** Nuclear incident at Three Mile Island, Pennsylvania. U.S. withdraws support for Somoza regime in Nicaragua, which falls. |
| **1980** Death of Marshal Tito, leader of Yugoslavia | **1980** Deng Xiaoping clamps down on democracy wall movement in China. U.S. attempt to rescue hostages in Iran fails. Iraq invades Iran, setting off Iran-Iraq War. Rhodesia becomes Zimbabwe, with Robert Mugabe as head of government. Smallpox eradicated worldwide. | |
| **1981** Communist government in Poland declares martial law. Greece joins the EEC. | **1981** Iran frees U.S. hostages. Anwar Sadat of Egypt assassinated by Islamic militants. | **1981** Ronald Reagan becomes U.S. president. United States launches first reusable space shuttle. |
| | **1982** Israeli invasion of Lebanon against PLO | **1982** Large-scale climate change attributed to El Niño |
| **1983** Lech Walesa, leader of Polish Solidarity trade union, wins Nobel Peace Prize | **1983** U.S. troops enter Lebanon as part of multinational force (MNF); suicide bomb attack on MNF barracks kills 239 U.S. and 58 French personnel; U.S. embassy also destroyed by a bomb; MNF withdraws from Lebanon | **1983** U.S. president Reagan launches Strategic Defense Initiative (Star Wars). U.S. invasion of Grenada. Argentina returns to civilian government. |

1975—

1980—

20th Century

| EUROPE | AFRICA AND ASIA | THE AMERICAS |
|---|---|---|
| | **1984** China designates Shanghai an open city to encourage foreign investment. Leak of toxic chemicals in Bhopal, India. | |
| **1985** Mikhail Gorbachev becomes leader of the USSR and announces an end to Soviet interference in Eastern European countries. Jacques Delors becomes president of the European Commission. | **1985** Economic sanctions imposed on South Africa by United States and Britain | |
| **1986** Libya blamed for terrorist bomb explosion in a West Berlin discotheque. Nuclear reactor explodes at Chernobyl in Ukraine. Demonstrations against Soviet rule in Latvia, Estonia, Lithuania, and Belarus. Portugal and Spain join the EEC; EEC countries agree to create a single European market by 1992. | **1986** U.S. air strikes on Libya. South Africa abolishes pass laws. | **1986** *Challenger* disaster: space shuttle explodes on takeoff. Irangate/Contragate scandal in United States. |
| **1987** Slobodan Milosevic becomes leader of Serbia | **1987** USSR forces begin to withdraw from Afghanistan. Japanese economy becomes second-largest in world. Robert Mugabe turns Zimbabwe into a one-party socialist state. | **1987** Costa Rican president Oscar Arias wins Nobel Peace Prize for establishing a peace plan for Central America |
| **1988** Strikes in Poland against government economic policies. Hungarian Communist Party replaces Kádár as leader. British prime minister Margaret Thatcher attacks plans for a "European superstate." Terrorist bomb kills 270 people on PanAm flight over Lockerbie, Scotland; Libyan agents believed responsible. | **1988** Ceasefire ends Iran-Iraq War | |
| **1989** Communist one-party rule ends in Poland. Latvia, Estonia, and Lithuania seek autonomy from Soviet rule. Hungary declares itself a democracy and allows East German migrants to exit to Western Europe. Anticommunist demonstrations in East Germany; border with West Germany reopened. Police suppress student demonstration in Czechoslovakia. Czech opposition forms Civic Forum and national strikes force resignation of communist government; Václav Havel elected president. In Romania, the Ceausescu regime falls. | **1989** Chinese government suppresses pro-democracy demonstrations in Tiananmen Square, Beijing. USSR completes withdrawal of troops from Afghanistan. | **1989** *Exxon Valdez* oil spill on Alaskan coast. U.S. troops land in Panama and capture General Manuel Noriega. |
| **1990** Reunification of East and West Germany. Elections in Hungary: communists lose power. Communist Party loses monopoly of political power in USSR; Boris Yeltsin elected president of Russian Federation on anti-Soviet program. Margaret Thatcher loses leadership of British Conservative Party; John Major becomes prime minister in her place. Lech Walesa elected president of Poland. | **1990** F. W. de Klerk becomes president of South Africa; Nelson Mandela released, ban on ANC lifted, and racial segregation laws begin to be dismantled | **1990** End of Augusto Pinochet's dictatorship in Chile. Sandinistas voted out of power in Nicaragua; Violeta Chamorro becomes first female head of state in Latin America. U.S. launches Hubble Space Telescope. |
| **1991** Slovenia and Croatia declare independence from Yugoslavia; Serbia attacks Croatia. Unsuccessful coup against Gorbachev by hardline communists; Communist Party outlawed; Russia, Ukraine, and Belarus form Commonwealth of Independent States; USSR abolished. Anticommunist revolution in Albania; aid from Italy prevents mass starvation. Chechnya declares independence from Russia. | **1991** Iraqi forces invade Kuwait but are expelled by the United States and its allies in Gulf War. Famine in Sudan. Military junta overthrown in Ethiopia. Somali president Siyad Barre overthrown; warlords take over. | **1991** Cutbacks in U.S. Strategic Defense Initiative. |

20th Century

| EUROPE | AFRICA AND ASIA | THE AMERICAS |
|---|---|---|
| **1992** Maastricht Treaty agrees plan for European monetary union. Boris Yeltsin elected leader of Russia. First noncommunist president of Albania elected. Truce between Serbia and Croatia; Bosnia-Herzegovina declares independence from Serbia. | **1992** Last Beirut hostages set free. United Nations forces intervene in Somalia. | **1992** Coup in Venezuela fails to overthrow government. Abimael Guzmán, leader of Shining Path guerrilla movement, captured in Peru. First "earth summit," in Rio de Janeiro, Brazil. |
| **1993** Czechoslovakia divides into the Czech Republic and Slovakia. In Russia, political opponents impeach Boris Yeltsin. | **1993** Israeli prime minister Yitzhak Rabin and PLO leader Yasir Arafat agree on Palestinian self-rule in West Bank and Gaza. Military government in Algeria blocks election victory by Islamic fundamentalist party; widespread killings begin. Eritrea gains independence from Ethiopia. Continued famine in Sudan. Democratic civilian government established in South Korea. | **1993** World Trade Center in New York bombed by Muslim group. North American Free Trade Agreement (NAFTA) creates free trade in North America. |
| **1994** Socialist Party led by former communists wins power in Hungary. Russian troops enter Chechnya to suppress independence movement. Channel Tunnel opens for rail travel between Britain and the European mainland. | **1994** Democratic elections result in first multiracial government in South Africa, led by Nelson Mandela. In Rwanda, government militia begin to exterminate some 500,000 Tutsis and government opponents. | **1994** Zapatista guerrilla group becomes active in Mexico |
| **1995** Austria, Finland, and Sweden join the European Union (EU) | **1995** Israeli prime minister Yitzhak Rabin assassinated by Jewish extremist. Ebola outbreak in western Zaire. | **1995** Peruvian Shining Path guerrilla movement ceases operations. Federal building in Oklahoma City bombed by American separatists. |
| | **1996** Truth and Reconciliation Commission set up in South Africa. Armed Muslim fundamentalist group, the Taleban, establish regime in Afghanistan. | **1996** Civil war in Guatemala ends |
| **1997** British scientists successfully clone a sheep, "Dolly" | **1997** Britain returns Hong Kong to China. Second "earth summit" in Kyoto, Japan. Petronas Towers, the world's tallest building, completed in Kuala Lumpur, Malaysia. Currency collapse in Thailand, Malaysia, and Indonesia. | |
| **1998** Five former Soviet bloc countries and Cyprus begin negotiations for future membership of EU | **1998** President Suharto of Indonesia forced to resign. Two U.S. embassies in Africa bombed by Muslim extremists. | |
| **1999** The euro becomes official EU currency. Poland, Hungary, and the Czech Republic join NATO. Serbia begins campaign of ethnic cleansing against Albanians in Kosovo; NATO airstrikes force Serbian troops to withdraw from Kosovo. | | **1999** Global economic crisis spreads to Latin America |

1995—

20th Century

# Glossary

**apartheid** an Afrikaans word for "apartness," used to describe the policy of formal racial segregation imposed by the white government of South Africa between 1948 and 1991. The policy classified people into four groups—white, black, Colored (mixed race), and Asian—and limited the civil rights and work and residential opportunities of non-whites.

**atom bomb** the earliest type of nuclear bomb, which utilized energy released by fission, or splitting the nuclei of plutonium or uranium atoms. The bomb was developed by the U.S. Manhattan Project during World War II.

**civil rights** the name given to the rights of an individual, particularly the right to personal liberty, freedom from injustice, and equality of treatment. Civil rights movements became prominent in the United States in the 1960s, when they opposed segregation and discrimination against black people. Other civil rights campaigns have campaigned to end discrimination against women and gay people.

**Cold War** the name given to the period of hostile confrontation (1945–1989) between the Soviet Union and its communist allies on one hand and the United States and its allies on the other.

**consumerism** a preoccupation with and inclination toward the buying of consumer goods, sometimes allied with a theory that the increased consumption of such goods is economically desirable. Consumerism emerged during the 1950s, when growing prosperity allowed ordinary people to buy consumer goods such as cars, vacuum cleaners, televisions, and fashionable clothes. The word consumerism is also used for the movement that grew up to protect the interests of consumers.

**counterculture** a culture that emerged in the late 1960s in the United States, mainly among young people who consciously rejected the values of established society with regard to matters of appearance and behavior. Members of the counterculture also distrust government and business, reject traditional relationships between men and women, and encourage an awareness of non-Christian paths to spiritual growth.

**Cultural Revolution** a movement launched in 1966 in China by Mao Tse-tung that aimed to revive radical fervor in Chinese communism. Many leading officials were replaced and a youth organization called the Red Guards was formed to promote the teachings of Mao. The Guards' activities disrupted society and industry so much that the Cultural Revolution was abandoned and Chinese society began to get back to normal after 1969.

**decolonization** the process of freeing colonies from imperial control to become independent countries.

**deforestation** the loss of woodland, mainly due to human activity such as the clearance of woodland for agriculture or the felling of trees for fuel and timber. Large-scale deforestation contributes to climatic change because forests convert atmospheric carbon dioxide into oxygen.

**democracy** a system of government in which a majority of citizens elect representatives to govern on their behalf.

**democracy wall movement** a movement that developed in China in 1979, when Chinese who wanted political reform began using a wall in Beijing to put up posters outlining their views. Similar walls developed in other cities but in 1980 the goverment banned all forms of prodemocracy agitation, including democracy walls.

**dirty war** the name given to the state terrorism carried out by the military regime in Argentina between 1976 and 1983, during which thousands of the regime's opponents were imprisoned without trial, tortured, or killed.

**earth summit** the name given to two meetings of world political leaders to discuss environmental problems. The first was in Rio de Janeiro, Brazil, in 1992, and the second in Kyoto, Japan, in 1997.

**El Niño** a Spanish phrase for "the Christ child," used to describe a regular disruption in the weather systems of the Pacific. Among the effects of the disruption is a warm ocean current that appears off the west coast of South America, usually soon after Christmas, from which the phenomenon derives its name. El Niño can have consequences all around the world, including extreme weather, ecological disasters, and serious crop failures.

**ethnic cleansing** a policy of removing an ethnic group from an area by violence, intimidation, or extermination, so that another ethnic group can occupy it. The term originated in the wars in the former Yugoslavia in the early 1990s.

**European Community** a political and economic grouping of European states, originally called the European Economic Community, created by the Treaty of Rome in 1957. In 1992, the Maastricht Treaty turned the European Community into the European Union and created closer links between the twelve member states.

**family planning** the use of contraception and sex education to limit the size of families.

**feminism** a belief that women are entitled to equal civil, legal, and individual rights as men.

**fundamentalism** an approach to religion that emphasizes adherence to basic beliefs and literal interpretations of scripture.

**glasnost** a Russian word for "openess," used to describe the increased freedom of political discussion introduced to the Soviet Union by Mikhail Gorbachev.

**globalization** the process by which all parts of the world become increasingly interconnected economically and culturally, regardless of national boundaries.

**global warming** a process that many scientists believe is gradually increasing the average temperature of the earth's atmosphere, largely due to the increase in the atmosphere of gases that trap the sun's heat close to the planet. The theory is challenged by scientists who argue that warm periods occur naturally.

**Great Leap Forward** a policy launched in China by Mao Tse-tung in 1958 to speed up economic development by a reorganization of industry and the creation of large farming communes. Within three years, the policy produced a slump in industrial output and food production; in the resulting famine, some 30 million people died.

**Great Society** the term used by U.S. president Lyndon B. Johnson to describe the goal of his social legislation from 1964 on.

**greenhouse gases** gases such as carbon dioxide and many pollutants that accumulate in the earth's atmosphere and prevent heat escaping into space, thus possibly causing the atmospheric temperature to build up. *See also* global warming.

**guerrilla warfare** a style of warfare adopted by small mobile groups of fighters who avoid direct confrontation with a more powerful enemy and rely instead on hit-and-run tactics, ambushes, and sabotage.

**green revolution** the name given to the introduction of new farming methods in the developing world encouraged by the United Nations in the 1960s and 1970s. Although agricultural production rose in numerous countries, the new methods were often expensive and thus unsuited to the long-term needs of developing countries.

**Hamas** a militant Palestinian organization that uses terrorist tactics to attack the state of Israel.

**international debt** the debts owned by countries to other countries, either because of direct financial loans or because of an imbalance in trade. The term is especially applied to the large sums owed by developing countries to the developed world as a result of loans made in the Cold War period. Many debtor nations now find it difficult to pay even the interest on the loans, let alone the capital.

**International Monetary Fund** an agency of the United Nations that uses its large financial reserves to help individual countries with problems caused by economic growth, unemployment, balance of payments, and debt.

**Internet** a worldwide electronic communications network that links computers and computer systems. The Internet has many commercial, academic, and recreational uses.

**iron curtain** a phrase coined by British prime minister Winston Churchill to describe the separation of western Europe from the Soviet bloc to the east.

**jihad** an Arabic word meaning "holy war" that refers to Islamic teachings about religious warfare against non-Muslims.

**junta** a Spanish word for a committee, usually applied to a small group, often of military officers, that seizes power in a country. Numerous Latin American countries were governed by juntas in the 1970s and 1980s.

**liberation theology** a form of Catholicism that developed in Latin America in the 1970s and argued that priests should actively promote the welfare and political rights of the poor despite the church's traditional allies among landowners and conservative elements in society.

**mixed economy** a term that describes either an economy that includes both private and state-owned businesses or one that is partially subject to government planning and partly left to the free market forces of supply and demand. In practical usage, a mixed economy is one in which state and private ownership, government planning, and market forces all play a major role.

**Moral Majority** a largely Baptist religious organization that emerged in the southern United States in the late 1970s to promote the moral regeneration of society through Christian fundamentalism and right-wing politics. The Moral Majority opposed abortion, feminism, and homosexual rights, and campaigned against pornography, crime, prostitution, and drug taking.

**multinational corporation** a company that has operations in a number of countries around the world, often to take advantage of cheap labor, materials, or transport costs.

Motor vehicle manufacturers, drug companies, and oil companies are typical examples. Multinationals often have a major impact on the economies of developing countries in which they operate.

**nationalism** a political belief that a people has the right to govern itself in its own country.

**neocolonialism** a situation in which a country continues to dominate a former colony, usually for economic or geopolitical reasons, as in continued European economic influence in Africa and Asia after decolonization.

**Pacific Rim** a geographic term for countries bordering on or located in the Pacific Ocean, used particularly in relation to the rapidly developing economies of Asia.

**perestroika** a Russian word meaning "restructuring" that refers to the program of political and economic reforms launched in the USSR by Mikhail Gorbachev after he became Soviet leader in 1985.

**referendum** an often national vote on a single political issue, particularly those involving major constitutional change.

**resistance movements** underground organizations in occupied or nearly occupied countries that wage secret campaigns of sabotage or guerrilla warfare against the occupation forces and their collaborators.

**rights politics** a term describing a political approach that emphasizes the fight for civil and human rights for groups that suffer discrimination, such as black people, women, gay people, and others. More generally, much of the developing world has seen long battles for human rights against authoritarian or colonial regimes.

**secularization** the process of reducing the role of religion in politics and national life, either through the adoption of formal legislation or more often through a gradual and general decline in the influence of religion in daily life and the political establishment.

**sovereignty** a country's formal political control over its own affairs and freedom from outside interference.

**space race** the name given to the intense competition between the United States and the Soviet Union to achieve breakthroughs in space exploration. The space race was given political urgency by the Cold War. The USSR took an early lead by launching the world's first artificial satellite in 1957 and putting Yuri Gagarin into orbit above the earth in 1959, but the United States achieved the goal of landing the first man on the moon in 1969.

**star wars** the term popularized by the media for the Strategic Defense Initiative

(SDI) proposed by U.S. president Ronald Reagan in 1983. The program aimed to develop space-based weapons, such as lasers, to shoot down intercontinental ballistic missiles, thus undermining the nuclear stalemate that existed between the United States and the Soviet Union. SDI never came to fruition, largely because of its vast cost.

**sustainable growth** a form of economic development that does not exhaust natural resources but instead is based on the exploitation of renewable resources.

**terrorism** the use of often indiscriminate violence or the threat of violence to obtain political or religious ends through acts such as bombings, killings, kidnaps, and hijacks.

**United Nations** an international organization set up in 1945 to replace the League of Nations as a means of resolving international disputes and avoiding military conflict. The UN consists of a General Assembly of representatives of all member nations; a Security Council, which includes six elected and five permanent members (the United States, the United Kingdom, Russia, France, and China); and a Secretariat, which administers the organization and is headed by an appointed secretary general. The UN also includes the International Court of Justice and a number of specialized agencies, including the World Bank, the International Monetary Fund, the World Health Organization, and UNESCO (the United Nations Educational, Scientific, and Cultural Organization).

# Further Resources

## The Political Debate 1960–1999
Brinkley, A. *Liberalism and Its Discontents*. Cambridge, MA: Harvard University Press, 1998.
Dutton, D.*British Politics Since 1945: The Rise,Fall and Rebirth of Consensus*. Malden, MA: Blackwell Publishing, 1997.
Padgett, S. *A History of Soviet Democracy in Postwar Europe*. White Plains, NY: Longman Publishing Group, 1991.
Karvonen, L.,and Sundberg, J. *Social Democracy in Transition: Northern, Southern and Eastern Europe*. Aldershot, UK: Dartmouth Publishing Company, 1991.
Milner, H. *Social Democracy and Rational Choice: The Scandinavian Experience and Beyond*. New York: Routledge, 1995.
Varson, A., ed. *Europe 1945–1990: The End of an Era?* New York: St. Martin's Press, 1994.

## Life in the Nuclear Age
Branch, T. *Parting the Waters: America in the King Years, 1954–63*. New York: Touchstone Books, 1989.
———. *Pillar of Fire: America in the King Years, 1963–65*. New York: Simon & Schuster, 1998.
Bundy, William P.*Tangled Web: The Making of Foreign Policy in the Nixon Presidency*. New York: Hill & Wang Publishing, 1998.
Evans, H., et al. *The American Century*. New York: Knopf, 1998.
Franeese, C. *From Tupela to Woodstock: Youth, Race and Rock-and-Roll in America 1954–69*. Dubuque, IA: Kendall/Hunt Publishing Company, 1995.
Wexler, S. *The Civil Rights Movement*. New York: Facts on File, 1993.

## China 1949–1999
Hunt, M. H.*The Genesis of Chinese Communist Foreign Policy*. New York: Columbia University Press, 1996.
Lawrence, A. *China Under Communism*. New York: Routledge, 1998.
Lieberthal, K. *Governing China: From Revolution Through Reform*. London: W. W. Norton & Co., 1995.
MacFarquhar, R., ed. *The Politics of China: The Eras of Mao and Deng*. New York: Cambridge University Press, 1997.
Zhang, Y. *China in International Society Since 1949: Alienation and Beyond*. New York: St. Martin's Press, 1998.

## Toward a United Europe
Dawson, A. H. *A Geography of European Integration*. New York: John Wiley and Sons, 1993.
Lubbers, R. *Europe: A Continent of Traditions*. New York: Cambridge University Press, 1994.
Nicoll, W. *Understanding the New European Community*. New York: Harvester Wheatsheaf, 1994.
Salmon, T. C., ed. *Building European Union: A Documentary History and Analysis*. Manchester, UK: Manchester University Press, 1997.
Urwin, D. W. *The Community of Europe: A History of European Integration Since 1945*. Reading, MA: Addison Wesley Publishing Company, 1995.
Wood, D. M. *The Emerging European Union*. Reading, MA: Addison Wesley Publishing Company, 1995.

## Latin America Since 1945
Cottam, M. L. *Images and Intervention: U.S. Policies in Latin America*. University of Pittsburgh Press, 1994.
Dominguez, J. I., ed. *Economic Strategies and Policies in Latin America*. New York: Garland Publishing, 1994.
Feitlowitz, M. *A Lexicon of Terror: Argentina and the Legacies of Torture*. New York: Oxford University Press, 1998.
Fraser, N. *Evita: The Real Life of Eva Perón*. London: W. W. Norton & Co., 1996.
Randall, L., ed. *The Political Economy of Latin America in the Postwar Period*. Arlington, TX: University of Texas Press, 1997.
Ward, J. *Latin America: Development and Conflict Since 1945*. New York: Routledge, 1997.

## Economies of the Pacific Rim
Collinwood, D. W. *Japan and the Pacific Rim*. Guilford, CT: Dushkin Publishing Group, 1997.
Cotterall, A. *East Asia: From Chinese Predominance to the Rise of the Pacific Rim*. New York: Oxford University Press, 1995.
Frost, L. *Coming Full Circle: An Economic History of the Pacific Rim*. Boulder, CO: Westview Press, 1993.
Morley, J. W., ed. *Driven by Growth: Political Change in the Asia Pacific Region*. Armonk, NY: ME Sharpe, 1999.
Simone, V. *The Asian Pacific: Political and Economic Development in a Global Context*. Reading, MA: Addison Wesley Publishing Company, 1994.

## Postcolonial Africa
Ayittey, G. *Africa Betrayed*. New York: St. Martin's Press, 1993.
———. *Africa in Chaos*. New York: St. Martin's Press, 1998.
Davidson, B. *The Black Man's Burden: Africa and the Curse of the Nation-State*. Times Books, 1993.
Gourevitch, P. *We Wish to Inform You That Tomorrow We Will Be Killed With Our Families: Stories From Rwanda*. New York: Farrar, Straus & Giroux, 1998.
Maier, K. *Into the House of the Ancestors: Inside the New Africa*. New York: John Wiley & Sons, 1997.

Waldmeir, P. *Anatomy of a Miracle: The End of Apartheid and the Birth of the New South Africa*. London: W. W. Norton & Co., 1997.

Welliver, T. K. *African Nationalism and Independence*. New York: Garland Publishing, 1993.

### Islamic Ferment

Al-Ashmawy, M. S. *Against Islamic Extremism*. Gainesville, FL: University Press of Florida, 1998.

Huband, M. *Warriors of the Prophet: The Struggle for Islam*. Boulder, CO: Westview Press, 1998.

Jansen, J. J. G. *The Dual Nature of Islamic Fundamentalism*. Ithaca, NY: Cornell University Press, 1997.

Naipaul, V. S. *Among the Believers: An Islamic Journey*. New York: Random House, 1982.

Sayyid, B. S. *A Fundamental Fear: Eurocentrism and the Emergence of Islamism*. London: Zed Books, 1997.

Tibi, B. *The Challenge of Fundamentalism: Political Islam and the New World Disorder*. Berkeley, CA: University of California Press, 1998.

Viorst, M. *In the Shadow of the Prophet: The Struggle for the Soul of Islam*. New York: Anchor Books, 1998.

### The Postcommunist World

Boettke, P. J. *Why Perestroika Failed: The Politics and Economics of Socialist Transformation*. New York: Routledge, 1993.

Dobbs, M. *Down with Big Brother: The Fall of the Soviet Empire*. New York: Vintage Books, 1998.

Maier, C. S. *Dissolution: The Crisis of Communism and the End of East Germany*. Princeton, NJ: Princeton University Press, 1997.

Remnick, D. *Lenin's Tomb: The Last Days of the Soviet Empire*. New York: Vintage Books, 1994.

———. *Resurrection: The Struggle for a New Russia*. New York: Vintage Books, 1998.

Rosenberg, T. *The Haunted Land: Facing Europe's Ghosts After Communism*. New York: Vintage Books, 1996.

### The World of Technology

Beniger, J. R. *The Control Revolution: Technological and Economic Origins of the Information Society*. Cambridge, MA: Harvard University Press, 1989,

Levinson, P. *The Soft Edge: A Natural History and Future of the Information Revolution*. New York: Routledge, 1997.

Pineira, R. J. *Breakthrough*. New York: Tor Books, 1999.

Schefter, J. L. *The Race: The Uncensored Story of How America Beat Russia to the Moon*. New York: Doubleday, 1999.

### The Natural World

Carson, R. *Silent Spring*. Boston, MA: Houghton Mifflin Company, 1994.

Daly, H. E. *Beyond Growth: The Limits of Sustainable Development*. Boston, MA: Beacon Press, 1997.

Karliner, J. *The Corporate Planet: Ecology and Politics in the Age of Globalization*. San Francisco, CA: Sierra Club Books, 1997.

Ponting, C. *A Green History of the World: The Environment and the Collapse of Great Civilizations*. New York: Penguin USA, 1993.

Tokar, B. *Earth for Sale: Reclaiming Ecology in the Age of Corporate Greenwash*. Cambridge, MA: South End Press, 1997.

### Problems for the Twenty-first Century

Castells, M. *End of Millennium*. Malden, MA: Blackwell Publishing, 1998.

Dobkowsk, M. N., ed. *The Coming Age of Scarcity: Preventing Mass Death and Genocide in the Twenty-first Century*. Syracuse, NY: Syracuse University Press, 1998.

Eldredge, N. *Life in the Balance: Humanity and the Biodiversity Crisis*. Princeton, NJ: Princeton University Press, 1998.

Jameson, F., and Miyoshi, M., eds. *The Cultures of Globalization*. Durham, NC: Duke University Press, 1998.

Robertson, D. S. *The New Renaissance: Computers and the Next Level of Civilization*. New York: Oxford University Press, 1998.

Schell, J. *The Fate of the Earth and the Abolition*. Stanford, CA: Stanford University Press, 1999.

Stephen, J. C. *Dragon Within the Gates: The Once and Future AIDS Epidemic*. New York: Carroll & Graf, 1993.

Utgoff, V. A. ed. *The Coming Crisis: Nuclear Proliferation, U.S. Interests, and World Order*. Cambridge, MA: MIT Press, 1999.

# Illustration Credits

# Index

Page numbers in *italic type* refer to illustrations and captions.

Page numbers in *italic type* refer to illustrations and captions.